The Witch's Guide to Haunted Objects

CHERISE O. WILLIAMS

BEYOND THE FRAY

Publishing

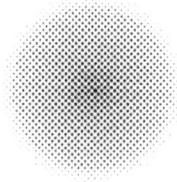

BEYOND THE FRAY

Publishing

Contents

Dedicated to the spirits in my life.

Introduction

The desire for a paranormal experience of your own makes the idea of haunted objects tangible and accessible. No need to travel to a potentially expensive haunted location when you can browse the internet or secondhand stores and find a haunting of your very own to bring home. However, by welcoming a haunted object into your life you run the risk of paying a price far higher than the cost of the item. The item could not be haunted at all, or worse, could be haunted or cursed with something you're not ready to deal with.

Objects hold such fascination because, technically, any object has the ability to become haunted. They're all around us and become haunted for many reasons. The past behind haunted objects tends to hold some mystery, as it's not always easy to figure out the history of objects, and people love a good mystery.

Take a look at shops on the internet, and you'll find no shortage of haunted objects. In fact, some websites even have haunted object categories. But are all of those objects truly haunted? There are lots of people who are more than willing to scam others for a quick buck or to get views on social media. I do believe there are legitimate haunted objects for sale; you just need to watch out for frauds and don't let yourself get scammed. Trust your intuition when purchasing any potentially haunted object and try to make purchases from reputable sellers. It's also a good idea to know what you might be getting yourself into when it comes to bringing a haunted object into your home. At the very least, you should know some basic protection and cleansing techniques. This is one of the reasons I wrote this book. I wanted to share creepy stories surrounding haunted objects, along with practical magickal tips for interacting with these items in a safe way.

Along with magickal techniques and advice, this book contains stories that I have heard of over the years, stories that others have told me of their personal haunted object encounters, as well as investigations I have conducted with various haunted objects.

Any stories that were submitted to me are written here just as they were emailed to me, except for a few minor spelling or grammar adjustments. In the case of stories that were audibly told to me, I wrote out the stories as closely as they were spoken in order to keep them in the storyteller's tone. For the online listings, I kept the text exactly as I found it except for a few minor spelling or grammar adjustments.

I've included transcripts of some of the Estes sessions I have been part of with several haunted objects. An Estes session is when one investigator listens to a spirit box while wearing headphones and a blindfold. The other investigator asks questions as the one listening to the spirit box calls out any responses they receive. The idea is that the person listening to the headphones can't hear the questions being asked, so it helps to remove some of the bias of what they perceive the spirits to be saying. In these Estes session transcripts, you will read the words of both the person asking the questions as well as the person repeating what they're hearing from the spirit box. In parentheses are things that the listener said on their own, or things they were experiencing in the moment. I included the sessions and responses just as they happened; however, I did omit questions and responses that didn't seem to make sense or weren't relevant.

There are many famous items that are haunted, such as Annabelle or Robert the Doll. I have chosen not to include some of these more popular objects within this book, as there is already a plethora of really great content surrounding them. Instead, I chose to share stories and objects that might be a little less known to the vast majority of people. Some of the stories included here are ones that I have come across over the years, but that I have no personal experience with. Others are ones that I have had the pleasure of interacting with or investigating personally, and finally, some of the stories are those that have been shared with me via others' firsthand accounts. In all accounts, I assume that the stories and information shared with me are factual.

The magickal information included here is beginner friendly. If you're curious about combining paranormal investigations with witchcraft and spiritual techniques, I recommend reading my book *The Witch's Guide to Ghost Hunting*. That book goes into great detail about various magickal techniques and how to pair them with traditional ghost hunting.

Chapter One

WHAT CAUSES AN OBJECT TO BECOME HAUNTED?

SPIRIT INHABITING THE ITEM

THERE ARE many reasons why an object might become haunted. One reason could be due to a spirit inhabiting the item, which is a conscious entity attached to the object rather than a residual energy. A spirit could be attached to this object willingly, because it was created or it was bound to it.

A spirit might willingly attach itself to an item as a way to weasel its way into people's lives unsuspectingly. Malevolent or trickster entities enjoy this method because it's almost like a way to sneak in through the back door. More than likely you're not going to knowingly invite a darker entity into your home. However, if the entity is attached to an antique item you just brought home, you'd have no idea. It's kind of like a loophole that allows the spirit to be invited into your life. This sounds creepy and messed up, but I want to remind you that this is actually pretty rare. Most entities that one would call a "demon" have far bigger and better things to be doing with their time than attaching themselves to a random object just to terrorize you. That's not to say it doesn't happen, it just doesn't happen as often as TV and Hollywood would want you to believe.

I want to mention that a lot of talk regarding haunted objects seems to happen around antique items; however, an object doesn't have to be old to be haunted. New objects have just as much potential for being haunted as older ones do.

Another way that a spirit might willingly attach itself to an object is if they were fond of the object in life. For example, perhaps there was a necklace that a woman's husband gave to her. In life, she absolutely adored the necklace, and it was her prize possession. Now, in death, the woman just can't let this piece of jewelry go, so she stays with the necklace. She goes wherever it goes in order to keep an eye on it. More often than not, if the spirit is content with where the object is and how it's being treated, they will be a friendly or unbothered spirit. However, if the spirit attached feels as though the object is being disrespected, they could potentially let you know they're displeased. This could show up as activity that some might claim to be "evil" and inaccurately associate it with a demon. Activity such as slamming doors, yelling on a spirit box or even scratching. Remember, just because a spirit is lashing out and the activity might seem aggressive or scary, doesn't automatically mean it's an evil entity or demon. If someone were treating an object with disrespect that you loved, you would probably lash out a bit too. Activity around an item does not only stir up when the spirit feels the item isn't being taken care of, but can increase when the spirit is bored. Some entities like the attention, and if they feel they're not getting the attention they want, they may feel inclined to kick it up a notch to get a rise out of you.

Sadly, some objects become inhabited by a spirit due to trauma. For example, if a man was smoking a pipe at the moment he was suddenly shot and killed, the trauma and quickness of his death could confuse his spirit, thus attaching or anchoring it to a nearby item, like the pipe. Thankfully, I believe these types of hauntings are rare. I don't believe it's the entire spirit of a person attached to an object during trauma, rather it is a fragment of their energy. This creates what I call a fragment haunting. But instead of it being a free-moving spirit found in a location, this spirit is attached to an object.

Some haunted objects are inhabited by a spirit willingly or accidentally, and others are created. There are theories that our thoughts can create a ghost, as well as a haunted object. On an episode of the television show *Kindred Spirits,* Amy Bruni and Adam Berry tried an experiment and created a name and entire backstory for a "ghost." At the location they were investigating there was a faceless shadow figure that had been seen by others. Amy and Adam had their suspicions that the spirit people were seeing was actually a collection of energy from previous investigators feeding into the idea of this shadow figure. Basically, the energy over time that others had projected had ultimately created this nameless entity. While at the location, Amy and Adam spoke about this entity as if it were a real person who had died, sharing details of its life and calling it by name. This experiment worked so well that their psychic, Chip Coffey, was picking up on these details during his reading of the location.

Similar to being able to create an entity using thoughts, a haunted object could be created in the same way. Think about it, you hand a group of investigators an object and tell them some wild backstory of the object and give them details of the spirit attached to it. In reality, there is no entity attached to this object, but nobody knows this except you. The investigators then spend time trying to communicate with this entity and object. They invest their thoughts and energy into this object, basically feeding the object. The next day, you give the object to a new group of investigators, telling them the same story, except now you may be able to include some anomalies that occurred with the last group's investigation, like receiving a name on the spirit box. Armed with this information, this second group investigates the object with as much energy and intent as the first. Thus feeding even more thought into the object. Before you know it, you have an actual spirit-like energy attached to this object. You and the other investigators have successfully created a haunted object. Unlike a conscious entity that is attached to an object, I feel that these types of mentally created hauntings require a frequent "feeding" of energy and thought in order to be sustained. The longer the haunting goes without being recognized or interacted with, the more it begins to fade away. While this experiment I just mentioned could be interesting to see play out, please don't be dishonest and lie to others about paranormal activity and hauntings.

Finally, an object may become haunted due to someone actively binding the spirit to an object. There are many ways to do this in witchcraft and magick, and many reasons why someone may choose to do so. At the end of the book I have included instructions for a very basic way to create a spirit vessel of your own.

RESIDUAL

A residual haunting occurs when energy gets imprinted into the environment and is then replayed or accessed at a later date. A large number of hauntings at locations fall under the residual category. These types of ghosts can't consciously interact with you, as they're not actually aware, they're simply replays of their former selves. The same can occur with objects. There might be energetic residue or memories attached to an object, but if you try to communicate with this energy, you won't get much response. For example, maybe you've acquired an old bed. Whenever you sleep in the bed, you have weird dreams of a ghostly woman, and sometimes the bed seems to shake or vibrate. You might try to investigate this bed, assuming it's haunted by the ghost of the woman from your dreams, but you don't get any response. This is because she's not consciously or actively haunting the bed, it's simply her residual energy attached to it that you're picking up on. Sometimes it can be difficult with objects to determine right away if it's a residual haunting or an active conscious haunting. Experience with energy work and trusting your intuition can come in handy to help you figure it out. Divination is an excellent way to help you determine the type of haunting.

How do some objects obtain residual energy? I'm not really sure, to be honest. Nobody is 100% sure how any type of haunting actually occurs, but there are theories or ideas. One being that an object was used frequently by a living person who was a projector, the types of people whose energy seems to radiate very strongly off them. The type of person who, no matter their mood, everyone else around can feel it, and it permeates the atmosphere. The objects that they frequently come into contact with could absorb some of this energy, potentially creating a residual haunted object. Another theory on how objects get residual energy attached is through trauma or other strong emotions. When trauma happens, a lot of energy is expelled into the environment all at once. Nearby items could potentially absorb that energy, thus creating a residually haunted object. Bursts of strong energy don't have to be limited to traumatic events. Moments like a wedding or the birth of a baby can be extremely joyful occasions that send bursts of happy energy into the world. Nearby objects could possibly absorb this energy as well.

Chapter Two

HAUNTED MIRRORS

THE HAUNTED CABIN MIRROR

Steve Hummel has always had an interest in paranormal topics and collecting odd or potentially haunted objects. This prompted him to start Archive of the Afterlife in 2011. Archive of the Afterlife is a museum in West Virginia that houses a wide array of haunted objects and oddities. He frequently takes these items to speaking engagements or to conventions, but you can also visit the museum for a tour or, for those brave enough, a paranormal investigation. I met Steve at his museum in the summer of 2022. I was particularly interested in hearing his stories surrounding a haunted or cursed mirror, as well as a potentially demonic doll (more on her later). Both of these items are kept in a room that Steve calls the Dark Room. This is a room designated for objects of a more sinister history or origin, such as items involved in exorcisms and demonic cases.

Steve told me about a few haunted mirrors in his collection and stated that two of the mirrors are kept in the General Relics room. These are haunted items that haven't posed a threat to anyone. In other words, these are the safe haunted objects. One of the mirrors in this room is called the Victoria Mirror. Steve's friend Vikki convinced him to buy the mirror after they noticed it for sale in the shop across the street from the museum's previous location. They felt oddly pulled towards the mirror, so they each took turns walking past the mirror to see if they could pick up on any energy. They both picked up on a feminine type of energy surrounding the mirror, so Steve purchased it to add to his collection.

The mirror I was most curious about was the mirror that is kept in a closet in the Dark Room. Steve states that not only is this mirror haunted or even potentially cursed, but that it could very well be a portal. The mirror was found in a derelict cabin deep in the woods of West Virginia. Steve is a member of a paranormal group called Paranormal Quest that has a very successful YouTube channel, and they do all kinds of investigations. One of these investigations was at the cabin, which Steve says was one of their more "interesting" cases that they did. They called the cabin the Cursed Cabin.

The cabin had initially been investigated by his friend Polly; then ten years later, Paranormal Quest and Steve investigated. The family who owns the cabin says it was built with logs from the property and says that once the cabin was built, any male in the family who lived in the cabin or stayed at the cabin would die after being there. The night that Steve investigated the cabin, it was pouring down rain. You couldn't hear much other than what was happening in the cabin as the rain pounded outside. While the team was setting up and recording some footage of the location, Steve noticed the mirror. It's a large antique mirror, roughly four feet tall, with an old dark wood frame around it. The mirror was, and still is, covered in a very thick layer of dirt and grime. Steve made a note to himself that he wanted to spend some time with the mirror that night; however, the cabin had other ideas. The living room ended up being quite active, with one of the team members, Jason, even getting scratched down the back by something unseen. Even though Steve didn't get to spend time investigating the mirror, he returned home, and thoughts of the mirror would creep into his mind. He couldn't get it out of his head. He contacted Polly, asking her if she could get ahold of the cabin owner to see if he could have the mirror. Months later, the owner finally returned Polly's calls, and she said that Steve was allowed to come get the mirror. The Paranormal Quest team returned to the cabin, on Halloween night no less, to investigate the cabin once more, and to leave with the mirror.

Steve believes that the mirror could potentially be so haunted due to all of the deaths surrounding the cabin where the mirror hung. In fact, one of the final deaths connected to the mirror was that of the cabin owner herself. Sometime after taking the mirror, Steve learned that the owner's son had gotten out of jail, come home, and shot and killed his parents. The cabin where the mirror had hung for decades was roughly two hundred yards from where they died. With all of the death and darkness surrounding the mirror, it's no wonder he keeps it locked in the Dark Room.

Multiple teams have come to investigate the museum since he's had the mirror. They've all indicated similar things that they've picked up on surrounding the mirror. To his knowledge, these teams have not met each other or have had contact with each other. These investigators say that the mirror has very heavy energy as well as portal-like indicators. When people are investigating the mirror, they claim to feel pressure on their chest, trouble breathing and dizziness.

I was drawn to the mirror but a little apprehensive to investigate it, knowing the history surrounding it. When you walk into the Dark Room, it's difficult not to be a little creeped out by the various dolls and other items held within. Perhaps the red lightbulbs, washing the room in a bloody hue, add to the effect. Walking across the creaky wood floor towards the closet in the corner, my gaze fell on the mirror that was leaning against the back wall of the closet. Dark, dusty and old, the mirror absolutely has a presence about it. I was investigating that night with my friend Sydney Wilson, and we decided to begin by investigating the mirror. We set up a laser grid pointing at the mirror, as well as a REM-POD in front of it. Shortly after setting up the equipment, the REM-POD went wild for a moment but then fell silent.

For the investigation, I was seated on the other side of the room, facing the closet with the mirror, and I kept seeing what I believed to be movement within the mirror. It looked almost as if something passed back and forth a few times, from somewhere deep within the mirror. While I was telling Sydney what I saw, a motion-sensor ball that was on the table next to me started to illuminate. The only way the ball will light up is if someone or something touches it. I was explaining to Sydney that what I was seeing in the mirror didn't look like a normal reflection, and the ball lit up a second time. To confirm that it was actually a spirit lighting up the ball, I waited until the ball stopped glowing and then asked the spirit on the count of three to light the ball up again. One...two...three...the ball immediately lit up. After that interaction, the ball stopped lighting up and didn't light up again.

We decided to try an Estes session with the mirror. I sat in the closet with the mirror while Sydney sat in a chair in the room with her back towards me. Sydney had the headphones on, listening to the spirit box, while I asked questions.

Cherise: Hello. I'm looking to specifically speak with any spirits or entities connected to this mirror.

Sydney: Hooha. Energy.

Cherise: Who am I speaking with?

Sydney: Out. Look around.

Cherise: Where are you?

Sydney: Twenty-seven. Come in now. Enter. (Sydney says she's feeling very cold.)

Cherise: You need to back away from Sydney; you aren't allowed to come into any of us.

Sydney: How?

Cherise: (I see movement in the mirror.)

Sydney: Fall in. Worry.

Cherise: Fall into the mirror?

Sydney: After you.

Cherise: No, thank you. What do you see right now?

Sydney: The end. (Sydney mentions again how cold she feels and that her chair felt like it moved a little bit.)

The responses from the spirit box seemed to end at that point. It really felt as if something was wanting one of us, or both of us, to come into the mirror with it. I made sure to set an energetic boundary, letting the entity know that we would under no circumstances be going into the mirror. It seems with some entities that it's their entire mission to get you to go into the mirror with them.

We then decided to switch places, with Sydney next to the mirror and myself listening to the spirit box.

Sydney: Is the mirror actually haunted?

Cherise: Scared moment.

Sydney: Is the scared moment trapped inside the mirror?

Cherise: Believe. (At this point it felt like something touched my chair. I immediately turned around to see if it was Sydney. It was not.)

Cherise: Chair. Do touch it.

Sydney: Are you touching Cherise's chair?

Cherise: Close. Are you there?

Sydney: I'm here; where are you? Are you in the room or the mirror?

Cherise: Talk to me.

Sydney: I am talking to you; can you hear me?

Cherise: Hello?

The session seemed to die down at this point, and the spirit went quiet. Perhaps because it couldn't hear Sydney talking or felt it wasn't being heard. Or maybe the entity didn't like the energetic boundaries that had been set. Either way, there was enough activity and bizarre responses surrounding the mirror that I do believe there is something very odd and paranormal going on with the mirror. I hope to make it back to the museum to investigate the mirror even more. With proper boundaries of course.

THE MIRRORS AT MCINTEER VILLA

Located in Atchison, Kansas, is the McInteer Villa. This beautiful brick home was built in 1889 for John McInteer. McInteer had moved to the United States from Ireland in the early 1860s, and he started a business manufacturing saddles and harnesses. The quality of his work was great, and his business became quite successful. His first wife, Alice, died in 1892, and he remarried to Anna Conlon. After Anna's and John's deaths, Anna's brother moved into the home. He and his family remained there until 1925, at which point the home became a rooming house for the next twenty-five years. Unfortunately, there isn't much information on the things that occurred during the rooming-house era or who resided there. After the home served as a rooming house, Ms. Isobel Altus, also known as Goldie, purchased and moved into the home. She would later pass away there. The rocking chair that she died in is still at the home today.

Presently, Stephanie O'Reilly is the owner of this large Victorian home. I had the pleasure of meeting Stephanie in March of 2022 when I was filming for a documentary of the home's haunting. Stephanie had been drawn to the home and purchased it with her father, who unfortunately passed away not long after. Stephanie has put so much love and care into this home, and she happily opened it up to paranormal investigators and tour groups. When talking with Stephanie, you can tell she not only cares about the property, but the spirits who reside within. The home is beautifully decorated with lots of antique furniture and art, including many old mirrors. In fact, during our investigation, we realized that literally every room of the home contained at least one mirror, a fact that became quite important during our stay. Many visitors to the home have claimed that the mirrors are quite haunted. One of these mirrors is located in what's called the Princess Room and is above the fireplace.

People claim that they have captured ghosts and apparitions within the reflective surface. During my time there, I didn't capture anything within this particular mirror. It's important to note that the mirror is an antique and has natural aging, which makes the reflection a bit muddled. Could it be the lighting in the room paired with camera flash and natural aging of the mirror's backing that causes people to see what they believe are ghosts? I do think this might explain some of the anomalies seen within this mirror (and other antique mirrors across the country), but I don't think it explains all of them.

Another of the villa's mirrors that has possibly captured a spirit within it is located in the dining room. This mirror is also above a fireplace; however, this mirror's reflective surface does not contain the aging like the one upstairs. Perhaps it's in part due to the clarity of the mirror that Stephanie was able to capture an extremely clear face within this mirror.

This photo was taken during an event at the villa. The man you see circled in the reflection of the mirror? Yeah, he wasn't there. At least, not physically and was not a living guest in attendance at the event. So then, who is it? Stephanie has her suspicions but isn't certain. The photo below shows a still image from Stephanie's security camera that was taken at about the same time as the ghost photo was taken. In this still frame, you can see the man with dark hair who was also in the mirror's reflection. This man was a living person in attendance at the event. However, in this still frame, you can clearly see that the ghostly man is not next to him; he only showed up in the photo taken of the mirror.

Located downstairs next to the dining room is another mirror above a fireplace. You will find this mirror in the front entry sitting room. This mirror does have some aging to it, which could explain away some of the ghostly sightings people are seeing in it. But like the mirror in the Princess Room, some people are certainly capturing very compelling images. Take this photo, for example. You see the person taking a selfie with the mirror, but in the mirror's reflection you see what almost looks like a woman with dark hair wearing a dress with a puffy sleeve.

Having personally spent time at this home investigating, I can say with 100% certainty that there is something extremely spooky going on with the mirrors.

DICKENS MIRROR AT THE PARKER HOUSE MUSEUM

During his second tour of the United States in 1867–1868, British writer Charles Dickens stayed at the Parker House Hotel in Boston.

At the time, this was one of the most luxurious hotels with oak walls, bronze detailing and crystal chandeliers. It even featured hot and cold running water, which Dickens mentioned in a letter home. The *A Christmas Carol* author stayed at the hotel for six months, and it was in his room, in front of the mirror, where he would practice his readings before performing them in front of live audiences.[1]

In the 1920s the hotel was torn down and a newer more modern one built in its place. Obviously, this meant the room that Dickens had called home for a period of time was also demolished. However, the door and the mirror can still be found today at the Omni Parker House. The large wall mirror hangs in the mezzanine of the hotel. Legend states that if you gaze closely enough at the mirror, you will see a ghostly image of Dickens, almost as if the hours he spent in front of the mirror years ago somehow imprinted his energy into the mirror's reflective surface. Others state that if you say "Charles Dickens" three times while looking into the mirror, you will see his image after the nearby elevator bells chime.

THEY TRAVELED THROUGH THE MIRROR

Many people believe and theorize that mirrors can act as a portal between our world and the world of spirits. It's one of the reasons some cultures cover mirrors with black cloth after someone dies, to prevent the souls from wandering and getting trapped. Every now and then we might get a glimpse from the mirror of these other worlds. For Fallon, she got more than her fair share of a glimpse. I normally keep any mirrors covered at night that face my bed. After hearing the following story, I will certainly keep up the practice.

It happened in the summer of 2015. I was twenty-one years old and living in an apartment complex in Cameron Park, California. I worked as a bartender at the time and would get home from work between the hours of midnight and 3:30 a.m.

On this particular night I got home from work around 2:00. I was exhausted and crawled into bed with my then boyfriend at the time. He was dead asleep, and I tossed and turned for what had to have been at least an hour. I don't know why I struggled so much to fall asleep because usually when I got home from work, I was out relatively quick. I suddenly heard the doorknob to our apartment twist and turn as if someone was trying to get in. I was petrified and didn't know what to do. I woke my boyfriend up, who also heard the noise, and we held each other and tried to remain as quiet as possible. The door flung open and slammed against the wall behind it. I could feel my heart beating the fastest it's ever beat in my life. For a second I thought I might have a heart attack. I heard footsteps approaching our bedroom, and then I saw a man and a woman both dressed in white standing in front of our bed with shotguns pointed directly at us. I thought for sure this was the end of us. That was it. My life was about to end. I lay paralyzed with fear as I stared down the barrel of the gun. Was this going to hurt? Would I feel anything? Why were they targeting us? I didn't recognize them. I looked over at my boyfriend, and he didn't seem as scared as I was. I didn't have time to ask him if he was seeing what I was, and even if I did, it wasn't a good time.

Before I could think any further, they both put their rifles down and began laughing hysterically. My eyes remained wide open as I watched their every move as they continued to laugh and walk around our bedroom as if they owned the place. I felt for a moment like I was in a Rob Zombie film in which the characters are tormented and laughed at. I felt humiliated. Before I even had time to fully process what just happened, I saw something moving inside our bedroom mirror located on the wall to the right of our bed. I couldn't quite tell if there was something there, or if the moonlight and my disoriented state of mind were playing tricks on me, or if there really was something there.

I couldn't believe what I saw next. A pair of pale white hands appeared out of the mirror, followed by long, frail arms, stringy, long dark brown hair and a corpse-like male figure dressed in overalls. It was a full-bodied apparition. It was at this moment that my fear that these were in fact spirits from another realm was confirmed. The beings I was seeing before my eyes were not living. I heard many stories before about mirrors acting as a portal to another realm. I never had any experiences of my own, but I did always find mirrors a bit creepy, especially at night. I found myself avoiding my own reflection or peering at them for longer than a brief moment in an effort to avoid the unthinkable on the off chance that the tales were real. It could also be thanks to the 2008 horror film Mirrors *featuring Kiefer Sutherland. Nonetheless, they never sit well with me.*

The spirit that climbed through the mirror walked directly in front of our bed and twisted his lanky limbs as though he were injured and made his way out of the room entirely. He didn't look at me or in my direction once. For the remainder of the night, I continued to experience the presence of strange entities dwelling in our bedroom. Some were aware of my presence and wanted me to know they were there, while others did not and gave the impression that they were residual spirits simply repeating history. I saw an elderly woman walk past us and heard her brush her teeth in our bathroom sink. A couple of teenage girls laughed at me repeatedly while attempting to hide behind our closet door and play some sort of twisted game of peek-a-boo. A few spirits climbed through the same mirror to the right of our bed and never returned. A little boy waved at me and said hello before disappearing as quickly as he appeared.

Ever since that night, I remain a firm believer that mirrors are a portal to another dimension. For whatever reason, that night I was chosen to see into the realm that lies beyond ours. The following morning, I asked my boyfriend if he saw the same things I did. I was too afraid to ask him in the moment out of fear that my voice would cause some sort of negative reaction from the spirits. I chose instead to remain a silent observer of the bizarre activity happening before me and save the questions for daylight. He said he didn't see anything, but that he could hear all of the same noises I did. He heard the teeth brushing, the girls laughing, the boy say hello, and the doorknob twisting. He did not see, but he heard.

I have been extremely sensitive to spirit energy ever since I was a little girl. I've lived in numerous haunted houses for the majority of my life and have had countless terrifying encounters with the paranormal, more so than the average person. Today I try to avoid intentional interaction with spirits due to the encounters I've had over the years. The story I just told is far from the only one, and believe it or not, it is one of the more tame. Regardless of what your beliefs are, there are spirits around us all the time. All it takes is one person telling the truth for ghosts to be real. The same goes for mirror stories.

– Submitted by Fallon Snead

CHARALAMBOUS AND BIRCH'S MIRROR

Joseph Birch and Sotiris Charalambous were roommates in London who acquired an antique mirror. A few days after hanging the mirror up, they both began to be woken up in the mornings, screaming in agony. It felt as if they were being stabbed all over their bodies. The excruciating pain disappeared as quickly as it had started. As if the physical attacks weren't enough, their apartment began to have issues as well. Their radiator broke, pipes would bang, and items would go missing. Eventually the activity escalated to more of a poltergeist-like activity, throwing objects around the rooms, and manifesting as shadows throughout the apartment.

Charalambous decided to paint the frame of the mirror silver, and apparently the entity attached was not pleased with this decorative choice. After painting the frame, the two roommates suffered horrific nightmares, and Birch even received scratches on his body.

It was at this point that the two had had enough. They listed the mirror for sale on eBay, along with a description of what they experienced, as they said it was only fair the future owner knew what they were getting into. Someone did end up purchasing the mirror; however, their identity and what they did with the mirror remains unknown.

THE HAUNTED MIRROR OF VERACRUZ, MEXICO

A man in Veracruz, Mexico, purchased an old ornate mirror despite the ominous warning from the shop owner that the mirror *must* be covered up every night. The man did as he was told and covered the mirror with a sheet when he got home that evening. However, he began to hear knocking. Knock...knock...knock... The knocking seemed to be coming from the mirror itself. Curiosity got the better of the man, and he removed the sheet to figure out what was causing the knocking sounds. When he removed the sheet, revealing the mirror's shiny surface, he was horrified to see a twisted version of his own reflection within the mirror. Despite himself standing still, his reflection was swaying side to side with an evil grin on its face. Terrified, he shakily reached his hand up to put the sheet back up, but it was too late. His ghoulish reflection reached through the mirror and tried to pull him in. The man was able to fight off his crazed reflection but not before being partially pulled into the mirror. Once the man broke free of the reflection, he ran from his home and didn't return until morning when it would be safe. The next morning, he returned, tore the mirror down off the wall, and burned it in a fire.

As far as I can tell, this story seems to be more of a modern urban legend than a true account of a haunted object. However, it does seem that with every tale and urban legend told, there is usually a bit of truth sprinkled in. So, who knows, perhaps this story has some truth to it.

YOU'RE MINE NOW

Sometimes it seems that the ghosts within mirrors make their presence known in unexpected ways, usually in mundane moments when we least expect it and our guards are down. I can't help but think that's done on purpose.

The year was 1987. I was ten years old and living in a half-double on Wyoming Street in Dayton, Ohio. I was a latch-key kid, both my parents worked, so I had to take care of myself. I came home from school that day, unlocked the door with my key that I had hanging on a lanyard around my neck, went in the house, and dropped my backpack on the floor. I ran upstairs and went through my parents' bedroom to get to the bathroom. The bathroom in that house was huge. It had black tiles on the floor that shined like glass, an old, huge, cast-iron, claw-foot tub that I used as my own personal swim-ming pool, a deep sink that was on a porcelain flower-stem-shaped stand, and a seashell-shaped toilet. Above the sink, on the wall, hung an old oval mirror. The frame of the old, oval mirror was brass. The whole mirror had to have weighed about one hundred pounds. We were told by the landlord that the mirror and bathtub were around one hundred years old. At the time, I didn't think anything of it. I just thought it was cool that they were that old...until that specific day.

That day, I was standing at the sink, examining my hands as I washed all of the remaining clay from art class out from under my nails and out of the creases of my fingers, when I felt a hand on my shoulder that started burning. I looked up, and there was a twisted face in the mirror, and I heard a deep, disembodied laugh and a voice saying, "You're mine now!" I screamed, ran out of the bath-room, across the top of the stairs, into my room, and slammed the door shut. I sat on the edge of my bed, shaking and crying, my shoulder still burning from the hand that had been there. I lowered the top of my shirt down off my shoulder, and there, where I felt the burning hand, was a red, hand-shaped mark with distinct finger-like imprints. I have been frightened of mirrors ever since.

– Submitted by Mary Bowling

MARILYN'S MIRROR

The Roosevelt Hotel in Hollywood is a historic hotel with more than one ghost story connected to it. One of the more infamous ghosts said to haunt the building is that of Marilyn Monroe. In life, Marilyn frequented the Roosevelt so often that she had her own suite there, suite 1200. Guests who have stayed in the suite, long after Monroe's untimely death, have reported seeing her apparition, particularly within the mirror. The hotel eventually removed the mirror from the suite, setting it up in one of the hallways. A housekeeper was cleaning the glass of the mirror one day when she saw a blonde woman in the reflection. She turned to say hello, assuming it was a guest, but when she looked, nobody was there. To this day people claim to see glimpses of Marilyn within the mirror. It goes without saying that Marilyn was a charismatic person; could it be that her energy somehow imprinted onto the mirror she gazed into from time to time?

DANIEL IN THE MIRROR

I truly don't know what it is about mirrors in bathrooms and why it seems that so many scary encounters occur there, but it's definitely not uncommon. Is it the fact our guards are usually down when we're in the bathroom? Is it the running water in the sinks that helps amplify spirit activity? Whatever the reason, it's unsettling.

So when I was living in Frostburg, Maryland, I had moved into my now wife's house. There was a child spirit there, or so we think. We would hear running in the halls at all times of the day, and running up the stairs, but one day after coming home from work, I got in the shower; when stepping out of the shower, I looked in the mirror ahead. Behind me, standing on the shower ledge, was a little boy with dark brown hair. I instantly turned around, but no one was there, then I turned back, and he was gone from the mirror. This was the only time this happened to me but was certainly the craziest experience I had with Daniel. By the way, Daniel is the name my wife and her friends gave him; they didn't know the spirit's actual name.

– Submitted by David Kneller

MY POSSESSION IN THE MIRROR

I was in middle school, and the movie *The Craft* had recently come out. A few friends and I loved the movie and took it as a "how to" of witchcraft, messing around with things we truly didn't know about (my current wiser witch self is shaking her head thinking about it all). We had attempted many séances and Ouija board sessions, among other things. Then one day, while hanging out in the park, we performed a "ritual," not really knowing what we were doing. I don't recall our exact words, but I do remember it had something to do with inviting a powerful spirit's energy to us.

We left the park shortly after, and as we walked back to my friend's house, I noticed I was feeling very weird and off, almost disconnected from myself. I wasn't really saying anything either, which for me is not the norm. My friends asked what my deal was, and I didn't really respond. I recall sitting in my friend's room, blankly staring ahead as they all talked and hung out. Suddenly, it felt almost as if a huge weight had been lifted from me as I came back into myself. I burst into tears because the feeling felt so odd and overwhelming. My friends were concerned, and so was I, but I didn't know what to say.

This whole period of time that I was playing around with energy and spirits, I began feeling pretty depressed and moody, which only escalated after the ritual. Sure, it could've just been typical young teenager stuff, but this all felt a lot heavier than that. What happened one night felt like confirmation that what was going on with me was much deeper and darker than typical teen angst. I was getting ready for bed and began to feel the same disconnected off feeling that I had felt after the ritual at the park. I tried to ignore this feeling as I got into bed. The last thing I remember is my head lying on the pillow as I closed my eyes. The next thing I knew, I was standing in my bathroom in the dark, looking at my reflection in the mirror. I don't know how long I stood there, staring blankly into my eyes. After some time, I lowered my head and closed my eyes. What I saw and felt when I looked up again still makes my stomach drop to this day. My reflection in the mirror was me, but it wasn't. It was like a distorted maniacal version of myself. Crazed and unfamiliar energy coursed through my body, which made the situation even more frightening. In an instant I knew intuitively that something was trying to consume me. I couldn't speak out loud, so in my mind I began screaming NO as I shook my head back and forth. I thought of everything positive and loving that I could think of, including my family, Jesus, Mother Mary and Heaven. I felt my spirit fighting with everything she had. The next thing I knew, I was sitting up on the edge of my bed. Other than being scared and exhausted, I thankfully felt like myself.

I do believe whatever or whoever the entity was that I conjured at the park and attached to myself stayed with me for many, many years after that. However, that night with the mirror I managed to set a clear boundary that it had no permission or right to possess or consume me. This entity contributed to a lot of darkness throughout my life until I was able to take care of it, but it never tried to take me over ever again. After the night with the mirror, I avoided looking at myself in a darkened mirror. To this day I avoid looking at myself in a mirror at night when I get up to use the restroom. The only time I gaze into a darkened mirror nowadays is when I'm fully prepared, centered and protected for a scrying session.

REFLECTIONS DOWN THE HALL

Mirrors themselves are considered portals and hallways a liminal space. What happens when a mirror faces a hallway? Perhaps a chance for a doorway or window into the liminal world.

I consider myself "sensitive," and I've had a few experiences involving mirrors, one of which was in the house where I currently live, where there is a lot of activity. One day I was standing in my bathroom with the door open and was applying some makeup, at which point I had that overwhelming feeling that someone was watching me. I didn't want to make too much movement, so I just glanced to the space in the mirror where I would be able to see anything behind me, including down the hall towards the living room. When I did this, I saw what I can only describe as dark gray smoke in a small cloudlike shape that was floating probably at chest height to me. Once I looked up, the smoke traveled quickly, all at once and with purpose, up the hall and turned into my daughter's bedroom. After that, of course, it disappeared, and I was just kind of in awe of it, questioning what I had seen.

Another story isn't really mine but rather my mother's and took place in my childhood home. We always kept a body-length mirror on the bathroom door, and when the bathroom door was open, you could watch yourself as you approached from the dining room. My mother told me that several times when she would approach this mirror to look at herself, she wouldn't be the only one in the mirror, but rather there would be a holographic-type old woman who would appear in the mirror almost over her. She remembers the old woman clear as day and said she was short, had white hair tied up, and a long gown. This was the same house where I saw my first full-body apparition, as well as many other ghostly stories.

– Submitted by Kyla Foster

BIHL MANOR

Bihl Manor is located in Fremont, Ohio. Not only is the home itself haunted, but inside you will find a mirror that is garnering some attention amongst investigators. The mirror, when purchased, wasn't known to be haunted, but with each investigation done at the home and around the mirror, it's clear there might be something going on with it.

The owner of Bihl Manor, Karlo Zuzic, found the mirror at an antique mall. He said the woman working there told him she had found it at an estate sale, but beyond that, the history of the mirror is unknown. Karlo purchased Bihl Manor in July of 2022 to fix up and live in, but he quickly discovered the home was inhabited by several spirits, both seemingly intelligent as well as residual. He decided to open up the home for private paranormal investigations, with profits from the investigations going to the home to restore it.

I investigated this home in November of 2022. Upon doing an initial walkthrough of the home, it was evident that there was some unique energy within this house, particularly on the second floor where the mirrored vanity sits in one of the bedrooms. The home feels very disorienting, and each corner of the home feels slightly different than the other.

We began our investigation by conducting a scrying session in front of the mirror. I went first and sat down alone in the room, facing the mirror. The room was slightly illuminated with a green light, just enough for me to be able to see my reflection and the room behind me. I slowly took a breath in and out as I relaxed into the session. Almost immediately, I noticed my face begin to shift a little, which is common with scrying. However, not long into my session, I began to feel a little off. Normally when I scry, I'm aware of myself and my surroundings even when I'm deep in the session, and I'm aware that the reflection in the mirror is myself, even if the image fluctuates or morphs a bit. But during this session, I began to feel separated from myself, like my reflection I was gazing at wasn't me at all but instead was a completely different person even though my appearance wasn't really changing at all. The sensation was more energetic than visual. I stayed in the session for a few more minutes, exploring the separation feeling while also trying to stay grounded and anchored in myself. I ended up shutting the session down not long after. When scrying, it's important to end and close the session if you ever find yourself not feeling right. Feeling disconnected from yourself, feeling as if you're being pulled or drawn into the mirror or generally just not feeling right are some key indicators that it's time to stop. I'm still perplexed by what was going on with that mirror. Was it the mirror itself causing me to feel this way, or was it the spirits within the home?

Other people who have come to investigate the manor have attempted scrying sessions with this mirror as well. Sally and Robert investigated the manor and had their own experiences with the mirror. Sally shared the following story with me:

My husband and I were at haunted Bihl Manor in Fremon, Ohio. Karlo Zuzic, the owner, asked us if we had ever tried "scrying." We had not. Karlo explained and suggested trying it in the upstairs bedroom. I tried it first. After several minutes, the image of a Down syndrome male approximately eighteen to twenty years old appeared before me. He was just looking back at me and then disappeared. I told my husband that he HAD to try it. He went in, sat there for a few minutes. An old woman with gray hair pulled back into a bun appeared before him. After about an hour, I went back to try scrying again. This time the image of an old gentleman appeared before me. He too just stared at me and then disappeared. It was quite an experience.

What makes Sally's story interesting is that during my investigation at Bihl Manor, we had picked up on the presence of an older gentleman as well as the woman with her hair pulled into a bun.

After my investigation, I couldn't get the mirror at Bihl Manor out of my head and wanted to get more information from the energy or spirit associated with it. So on the evening of December 11, 2022, I conducted a distance Estes session with Karlo and his friend Brian. Normally an Estes session is done with the investigators in person with each other; however, it can be done via distance as well. I've had previous success with distance Estes sessions, where myself and another investigator aren't physically together but are instead on video call, so I was confident this would work, and I believe it did. I called Karlo on video chat, and we decided Brian would be the one to "go under" first. He put the headphones on, and our session began.

Cherise: When I was at the house doing a scrying session with the mirror, I felt really weird; do you know why?

Brian: My sister. My suggestion.

Cherise: What's your sister's name?

Brian: Yeah.

Cherise: Is your sister the woman that has been seen in the mirror and in the house?

Brian: Deny it.

Cherise: Who is the woman that people have seen at the house and in the mirror?

Brian: Sit down, bitch. (Karlo was standing at this point. Brian and I were both sitting. Karlo sat down.)

Cherise: Where did this mirror come from?

Brian: Baker. It's a story.

Cherise: Did the mirror belong to a man or woman? Maybe a married couple? (During my investigation of the home, I felt a married couple energy in the room with the vanity.)

Brian: Previously.

Cherise: Yes, who did the mirror belong to previously?

Brian: Yeah.

Cherise: Who is attached to this mirror?

Brian: It's me.

Cherise: Who are you?

Brian: ...

Cherise: Are people safe to scry with the mirror?

Brian: Good morning, it's cold. Sunday. (It was in fact cold and a Sunday; however, it was evening for us.)

Cherise: Can you see me? Or Brian and Karlo?

Brian: Ain't nothing.

Cherise: Do you see the mirror?

Brian: Nothing. (At this point Karlo heard what sounded like an electrical "chirping" sound, as if a piece of equipment was going off; however, there was no equipment turned on other than the spirit box.)

Cherise: Are you inside the mirror?

Brian: ...

At this point we pulled Brian out of the session, and Karlo put on the headphones.

Karlo: I see you.

Cherise: Who is attached to the mirror? Can we talk about the mirror?

Karlo: Steven. Sixteen. Yes. (The name Steven came through on the spirit box during my previous investigation of the home.)

Cherise: Steven, do you have a last name?

Karlo: Home. I'm in the light.

Cherise: Are you attached to the mirror?

Karlo: It's fine. Hiding.

Cherise: Are you hiding in the mirror?

Karlo: Stop asking.

Cherise: Why?

Karlo: He's gone. (Karlo says a new female voice comes through.) Hello, yes? Fifteen.

Cherise: Are there now fifteen spirits?

Karlo: It's cold. Fifteen. Seven. Ten.

Cherise: Is the mirror a portal?

Karlo: (Karlo says a laugh came through.) It's cold. I'm over here.

Cherise: Is the mirror a portal?

Karlo: YES. Not happy.

Cherise: Who isn't happy?

Karlo: Say it.

Cherise: Who isn't happy?

Karlo: You better bail.

Cherise: Should we be concerned?

Karlo: It was here...down here...

Cherise: Where is "down here"?

Karlo: I'm looking at you, right here.

Cherise: (At this point I was hit with major déjà vu but couldn't pinpoint exactly what, and I said so out loud.)

Karlo: Don't say it.

Cherise: So you can see me? Or is it the guys that you see?

Karlo: So? (Karlo says a woman laughed.) Most definitely disturbed. (He says a growl comes through.) I'm done. Good (followed by another laugh).

Cherise: Why don't you want to talk about the mirror?

Karlo: ...

Cherise: Do you want to keep the mirror a secret?

Karlo: ... (He announces nothing but static is coming through, and he removes the headphones.)

This session, like most Estes sessions, left me with more questions than answers. However, when I pair the responses we were getting with my intuition, I feel as if the mirror is in fact a portal of some sort. At different times during the session it felt like we were hearing pieces of a conversation between a spirit or two. Almost as if one spirit would try to talk, or want to talk, but as soon as information about the mirror started to come through, a spirit or entity would shut the conversation down. Intuitively, it feels as if there is at least one spirit or entity attached to the mirror who is controlling the situation. This being feels masculine and feels as if he's nervous that if we find out who he is or that the mirror is a portal, Karlo may try to have the mirror shut down, sealed or even removed. I think the experiences and story with this mirror are just beginning to unfold, and I'm looking forward to exploring it more. I'm not entirely sure if the information we did get that seemed related to the mirror are actually bits of information for the mirror. For example, is someone's sister really the woman who has been seen in the mirror, or is she someone connected to the house itself? Is the name Baker that came through perhaps the last name of the previous owners? I'm not sure, but I believe more of this mirror's story and history will be revealed in time.

BRIAN'S PORTAL STORY

Brian Barnett is a paranormal investigator who shared with me an interesting experience he had involving a mirror while investigating his cousin's house.

On September 15, 2013, I had a team over to my cousin's house, as she was having activity in the home and asked if I would come investigate. In the picture below you can see the camera angle is on the two mirrors that are located on the west wall of the bedroom. Notice the time is 9:17 a.m. It is these two mirrors (mainly in the left one, which is an antique mirrored dresser) that have shown a lot of activity. Both these mirrors are on an outside wall, meaning the other side of the wall is actually outside. Another note, this side of the house is facing the Sandusky River in Fremont, Ohio.

Review the area in this before picture at 3:52:07 a.m., within the red circle.

```
2013-09-15 AM 03:52:07
CH 1
915035156.avi
```

In the snapshot of one second later, there is a light anomaly that flies into the mirror and seems to go farther into it.

```
2013-09-15 AM 03:52:08
CH 1
915035156.avi
```

Brian stated that he's not entirely sure what that light anomaly was. He says that what makes it unique is that he actually saw the light with his own eyes, which removes the possibility of it simply being dust or a bug on the camera IR light. Brian brings up an interesting theory regarding the placement of the mirrors. The mirrors he was investigating are placed against a wall that the other side of the wall is the exterior of the house, which happens to face a river. There are theories in the paranormal field that natural bodies of running water, like a river, enhance paranormal activity or even act as a means of spirit transportation. If that is true, could the fact that these mirrors are backed up to a river be contributing to the paranormal activity? In a sense, the mirrors act as both an energy enhancer or even a portal for spirits connected to the river?

OLD LADY IN THE MIRROR

Bathrooms aren't the only time that we have our guards down with unexpected ghostly mirror encounters. At night while falling asleep or just after waking up, when we're feeling drowsy, is a perfect time for us to see glimpses of the otherworld.

When I was young, my parents were going through a rough patch when I was in sixth or seventh grade, and my mother was staying at an old house down the street. It was old, well kept, and the antiques inside looked like a time capsule from the previous owners or tenants. It wasn't a scary home, but I did sense two distinct energies. One was an older gentleman on the first floor in, like, a parlour/office area that I had to pass through to get to the bathroom. I wasn't afraid, really, but it always felt like I was disturbing a very busy working person if ever I had to go through the room. On the upstairs floor, where the bedrooms were, I could sense the presence of an older woman. She seemed nice, I was uneasy at the feeling of being watched, but wasn't afraid. More sorry that I was intruding...

On one of my first nights there, I was either trying to fall asleep or woke up in the middle of the night to see with my eyes, but in the mirror only, the figure of an older woman, grey or white hair cropped short with curls, with glasses standing by the bed. I did not see the figure with my own eyes standing in the space, but only reflected in the mirror. The mirror was an old-fashioned standing mirror that could swivel vertically. After that, every night I would spin it to face the wall and put a blanket over it. I would remove the blanket and reset it when I left to go to school. I guess all the woman's belongings were there. I felt bad about moving things out of place...if that makes any sense.

– Submitted by JL

SCRYING AT THE VILLA

I had a very unsettling scrying moment when I was filming a documentary at the McInteer Villa. During one of our nights investigating, we conducted a scrying session in a very small room that had multiple mirrors hanging on the wall, including a traditional black scrying mirror. I was to lead the sessions, one each with fellow investigators Nat and Eliot.

Eliot and I began the first session. Sitting in the darkened room with a single candle in front of the black scrying mirror, I explained how the session worked. Both Eliot and I gazed into the mirror at the same time. While I looked in the mirror, I saw the image of an elderly man in my mind's eye. Eliot mentioned seeing what he thought was an older male behind my shoulder. He also noted seeing what appeared to be a pale misty-type figure move from one mirror to the next. Our cameraman and director, later revealed that during this session, he suddenly became extremely exhausted and almost dozed off while standing up and filming, which he thought was quite odd.

After Eliot's scrying session, it was Nat's turn. We sat down in the chairs across from the mirror, the candlelight flickering in the mirror's darkened surface. I again explained how scrying worked, as this was Nat's first time, and told her how the session would go. Scrying can sometimes take a lot out of me energetically, so for this session, rather than participating, I was simply observing and leading. This extra awareness I had available during this session ended up being a very good thing. Nat began her scrying session. Not long after her gazing into the mirror I started to sense an energy shift. I didn't say anything at first, simply observed; however, I was beginning to get a little worried. Nat's energy and the energy of the room had changed even more now. Several minutes passed, and Nat's gaze began to become more and more intense. It was then that she asked me if she should be feeling like she should go *into* the mirror, almost like something was pulling her in or inviting her. I immediately told her no, and it was at this point that I pulled her out of the session and closed down the mirror. She said she was feeling very weird and not quite like herself, so I quickly took us outside to cleanse and ground.

Standing on the freezing porch with the wintry air billowing around us, I had her take several deep breaths as I removed any energy trying to stick to her, as well as cleansed and strengthened her aura. I myself walked out into the snow so I could place my hands on a tree while I took some grounding breaths. Eventually Nat began to feel more like herself again, although I think we were both a little shaken from that experience. The energy shift that we had both felt was intense and unnerving. Looking back, and had I known what was actually haunting this home, I never would have had someone try scrying there for the first time.

Through our investigation and the experiences we had, we concluded that the mirrors throughout the home play a big factor in the haunting of McInteer Villa. This experience is a good reminder for you that if at any point you're conducting a scrying session and you feel as if your energy is being separated or pulled into the mirror, end the session immediately. At no point should you feel disconnected from yourself. Remember, you are in control.

HOW TO LOCK A MIRROR

I always recommend spiritually sealing, locking or securing the mirrors in your home regardless if you think they're haunted or not. Even if the mirror hasn't displayed any suspicious spirit activity, it's believed by many that *any* mirror can act as a portal or window from our world to others. By protecting the mirror energetically, you can hopefully help prevent anything from spying on you or entering your space. I especially recommend sealing the mirror if you suspect paranormal activity associated with it or if you'll be using the mirror in any magick or spirit communication.

There are several ways to seal and lock a mirror; listed below are a few of my favorites. You can choose one of these options, or do a combination of them. I suggest resealing your mirrors a couple of times a year. If it's a particularly active mirror, you might need to cleanse and seal the mirror more often. Please only cleanse, protect and seal mirrors that belong to you or that you have permission to work with.

- Draw a sigil or protective symbol on the back of the mirror with marker, pen or paint.
- Sigils are magickal symbols that can be utilized for a wide variety of things. One of which is protection. You can create your own sigil or use one you find in a book or online. If sigils aren't your thing, you can use whatever symbol you view as protective. For example, a cross, a pentagram, or even a simple X. If you're curious about working with sigils, especially in regard to paranormal investigations, I recommend reading my book *The Witch's Guide to Ghost Hunting*. There is a chapter devoted to sigils, including how to create them and use them for ghost hunting and spirit communication. As you draw the symbol on the back of the mirror, you want to be imbuing the symbol and the mirror with the energy of protection, a knowing sense that once the symbol is drawn, it will prevent anything unwanted from coming through the mirror. You might even say so out loud, speaking it into existence.
- Draw a sigil or protective symbol on the corners of the glass.
- This is similar to drawing the symbol on the back of the mirror; however, this also seals the front. Personally, I like to draw a symbol on the back of the mirror and the front, if I can. If I am only able to seal one side of the mirror, I make sure to do the front. If the mirror belongs to you, you can certainly draw the sigil on the glass with a marker or paint,

but using your finger is recommended. You can either use your finger as is, or you can dip your finger into protection water (recipe below) before drawing the symbol on the glass. As you draw your symbol on each corner of the mirror, going in a clockwise direction, you want to speak out loud your intentions of protection and boundaries.

- Wash the mirror with protection water.
- Utilizing this water will not only help protect and seal the mirror, but it helps cleanse the mirror of any previous energies. This is particularly good to do if you recently acquired the mirror (secondhand, antique or brand new). To create protection water, you will need water, a pot, stove, rosemary and clove. You really don't need much water; a cup should do. Obviously, if it's a very large mirror and you're cleansing the whole thing, you might need more. Put the water into a pot and heat to just about boiling. Add in a few cloves and a sprig of rosemary (fresh or dried). Let the mixture simmer for five minutes. Remove from heat and allow to cool before using. You can dispose of the herbs and any leftover water by pouring it outside next to your back door.
- Wash the mirror with moon water and rosemary (if using the mirror for scrying or spirit communication).
- If your intention is to create a mirror that will be used for spirit communication, scrying, or other magickal purposes, you can use a moon water and rosemary mixture. This water will help to amplify the spiritual energies of the mirror while also providing protection. Similar to the protection water, you don't need much. Take about a cup of water and a sprig of rosemary in a pot on the stove and allow to simmer for five minutes. Allow the water to cool a bit before transferring it to a jar with a lid, then place the jar

outside under the moonlight. Any moon phase will work, but the dark moon or full moon is best. I recommend leaving the water outside through the night, or at least for a few hours. Once you bring it in, wash the mirror with the intention and energy of protection and enhancing spiritual and intuitive energies. If your mirror is specifically for spirit communication, magick or scrying, keep the mirror covered with a cloth when not in use.

Chapter Three

HAUNTED DOLLS

BETTY THE DOLL

BACK IN 2020 I got the idea to conduct an experiment with a haunted object. I thought it would be fun and interesting to see if more than one person could have the same experiences with the object, without knowing what the other one had experienced. I reached out to my friend Amanda Paulson and asked if she wanted to do the experiment with me, and she was all for it. We thought this experiment would be extra compelling, as Amanda is in Washington State and I'm in Ohio. How cool would it be to have similar paranormal experiences on opposite ends of the country?

We set out searching for our haunted object. We found all kinds of options on eBay and Etsy, some of which we actually felt could be haunted, but a lot of them almost seemed too good to be true, or they were super pricey. We thought a big red flag for if an item was actually haunted or not was if the seller was charging a lot of money.

For example, there were so many listings saying how haunted the item was and that the seller couldn't possibly keep it any longer and needed it gone as soon as possible. But then they were selling the item for a pretty hefty price tag, far more than the item was actually worth.

But then we found Betty.

Betty was listed for $13 on eBay. This price point made us feel like she was more legit, as if the person selling her literally just wanted her out of the house and wasn't looking to make a profit. The fact that the account didn't have any other haunted objects for sale was another good selling point for us. Clearly, this person wasn't trying to make a bunch of money listing items they claimed were haunted.

Betty could actually be legit.

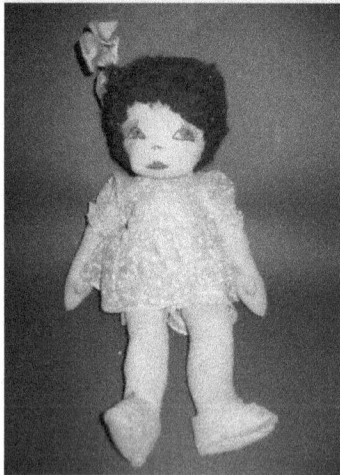

Haunted Spirit Vessel Paranormal Creepy
Dead Betty Doll Possessed Beware

The listing had quite the description:

Please be cautious if you bid on this doll, it is possessed and haunted. I acquired it in my neighborhood at an estate sale where the husband took his own life after the tragic death of his beloved wife. It came inside a trunk with some other items I wanted but had to take the whole thing, so that's when this treacherous doll came into my life. The first thing I noticed is that when I initially picked her up to look her over, I immediately began to feel nauseous. I put her in my garage and didn't think twice until a few days later she somehow wound up in my laundry room. I live alone, so did not put her there myself!

I put her in a box of items I was taking to a local thrift shop for donations, and while on my way to the thrift store, I was involved in a freak car accident. I was uninjured, but I am convinced this doll made it happen. I never made it to the thrift store but told some friends about what had happened. My girlfriend dabbles in paranormal and took the doll home with her. She quickly brought it back and said it was possessed by the dead wife of my neighbor. She told me she swears it whispered to her, "I will never die."

My cat hates it and runs away from it if it is in the house. This doll has been known to knock other items off the washing machine, etc. She is only 15 inches long yet, she holds the soul of a full-grown woman. She is made of cloth, which is well stained from who knows what. She wears a dress and pantaloons and little felt shoes. The shoes are probably felt so she can't be heard when she wanders around your house at night. Just look at that forlorn face of hers. To me, she appears to be looking up to her left, plotting her next move. Her arms and legs are held onto the body with buttons. I'm sure this was a super cute doll at one point, but over the years she has gotten herself in to too much no good and has become something I want gone ASAP. I threw her into the trash can outside, but the day after the trash had been picked up, she was in my backyard...Um, you gotta go, baby girl.

The neighbor woman who passed was named Betty (her husband was Ed). Betty had taken a fall, had a cracked skull and a stroke, and never regained the ability to walk or talk. She could grunt though. I think Betty has come back in the form of this doll to make her voice heard. So now I refer to this doll as "Dead Betty." Would you like to be the new caretaker of Dead Betty? Please drop in a bid. Trust me when I say I will gladly take her to the post office the second you have completed payment for her!

While the description in the listing was quite detailed and even humorous at times, we actually believed it to an extent. It did sort of sound like someone who was genuinely at their wit's end of having this haunted item in their home. We bought the doll outright without even bidding.

We decided that the doll would go to Amanda first, and that she would spend one week with Betty. Amanda would make notes of any activity that might occur as well as actively investigate the doll with various methods. She would not tell me anything that she was experiencing and, after a week, would send the doll to me. Then it would be my turn to see if any activity occurred and to actively investigate the doll. We had decided that we would do a few experiments the same, such as running the spirit box and asking questions, as well as our own experiments. Amanda with a pendulum and me with tarot cards. We made sure to record our interactions with the doll to put on our YouTube channels. After we each spent a week with the doll, we sent a video to each other where we shared our findings to see what correlated. We then did a video call together and conducted a distance Estes session, armed with the information we both got from our time with Betty, and asked some more questions.

AMANDA'S WEEK

As Amanda opened the package and got her first impressions of Betty, she noted that the doll was very dirty with abandoned-building vibes and lots of water stains. She mentioned feeling like the doll was watching her and that she had a nervous butterfly in her chest. It was at this point that Amanda looked at her Apple Watch and noticed that her heart rate had risen almost 20 points since opening the package of the doll. As Amanda was picking up on some irritation coming off the doll, she felt a hot energy on her back.

Amanda started her first investigation with Betty by doing a pendulum experiment, which she was recording. While she was explaining about the pendulum and what she was going to do, she began to hear weird noises down the hallway. This is intriguing considering what I would experience when I had the doll at my house. Amanda began her pendulum session, utilizing a pendulum board that had different emotions listed on it. The pendulum can swing to whichever word it wishes to convey. Amanda asked Betty what she believes is awaiting her on the other side, and the pendulum swung to the word "disappointed." At this moment, the temperature on the EDI+ meter Amanda had set out changed from 66.5 degrees Fahrenheit to 66.6. Feeling a little nervous, Amanda asked if the spirit attached to the doll was really an elderly woman. The pendulum indicated no. Not much more came through during that session, so Amanda ended it. Later that night, a shelf fell off Amanda's wall.

Amanda waited a couple of nights before actively investigating Betty again. One of those nights she felt extremely sick for no apparent reason. Perhaps it was the fact that she had placed Betty in her bedroom, near her bed.

The next investigation Amanda did with Betty was an EVP session; however, she didn't record any potential voices. She then attempted running the spirit box and asked how old the spirit was. The answer of "twenty" possibly came through, but was silent after that. Amanda ended the session.

Between her intuition, the responses she got from her investigations of the doll, as well as the other things she experienced during the week, Amanda's final impression was that the doll was not necessarily a human spirit and that the doll acts almost like a portal. After having multiple nightmares that week, Amanda happily packaged Betty up and sent her my way.

MY WEEK WITH BETTY

I received the doll on a Saturday, and my kids and husband were at home, so my house was noisy. I decided to open the package in my car in the church parking lot down the street so I could record the video in peace. Upon holding the doll for the first time, the impression I got was that she definitely gives off a vibe or a type of energy. Betty feels surprisingly heavy for being a doll made out of fabric, presumably filled with stuffing. Before I received her, I was intuitively picking up on something being inside her. Like there was something mixed within the stuffing. Perhaps Betty was a poppet (a spiritual or magickal doll) with locks of hair or something else inside her. While holding the doll, checking her out, I felt emotional touching her, almost like I wanted to start crying. This was several years ago, and I have since learned that when I'm feeling that type of overwhelming emotion that makes me want to cry, it's because I'm in the presence of a very strong and powerful spirit. Based on my initial impressions and feelings about the doll, when I came home, I decided to keep the doll on my altar, sitting in a circle of salt. I felt it best to try to contain this doll's energy. I don't think she liked that.

My first investigation with the doll was the day after receiving her. Since my kids and husband were home again, I did this session in my car in the church parking lot. I conducted an EVP session but had no results. I then tried using the Necrophonic app without much luck, so I tried my actual spirit box. But again, I had no luck or clear responses. I was feeling very frustrated with this session, which was a feeling that would become quite common as I interacted with the doll throughout the week. Taking a deep breath to try to calm my irritation (which, looking back, wasn't my own irritation but instead the irritation I was channeling from the spirit), I decided to try the Necrophonic app one last time.

Cherise: Did you die of natural causes?

App: I need help.

Cherise: What do you need help with?

This was about all that came through coherently, and I found myself getting more and more irritated and angry. I couldn't tell if it was gibberish that was coming through or if there were too many spirits trying to speak at once.

Cherise: Either there is nothing coming through, or there are too many spirits trying to talk. Are there multiple spirits attached to this doll?

App: There is. Yes.

Cherise: How many spirits or entities are attached to this doll?

App: Three.

Cherise: There's three spirits attached to this doll?

App: No.

It was around this time I began to think that maybe there was some trickster energy attached to the doll that was messing with me. I closed the session, went home, and returned the doll to her circle of salt.

The next session I had with the doll was a couple of days later, this time at home. I ran a digital voice recorder as I did a tarot reading for the doll. I asked how the doll was feeling in that moment, and pulled the Six of Wands. To me, this indicated that the spirit was feeling like they were getting their moment of recognition; they were liking the attention they were receiving. I asked who the spirit was when they were alive, and pulled the Knight of Pentacles. I knew the listing said the spirit was an elderly woman, but to me, the energy surrounding the doll didn't feel like that was correct. The Knight of Pentacles seemed to indicate a more masculine energy. When I asked why the spirit was attached to the doll, I pulled the Devil card. While, yes, this could possibly indicate that the spirit attached to the doll is malevolent, typically when I pull the Devil card in regard to a haunting, it is an indicator that the spirit or spirits feel bound or tied. Which, if the doll was indeed used as a poppet of some sort, it would make sense that the spirit felt tied to the physical doll.

At this point, I ran the Necrophonic app again. Almost immediately the word "secrets" came through. However, I quickly found myself getting irritated again and felt like too many spirits were trying to talk at one time. I set a boundary, stating that I was only trying to communicate with the spirit or entity attached to the doll. I asked if they understood, and heard "okay" come through the app. Again, I asked how many spirits were with the doll and got more random numbers. It was at this time I began to think that the doll was actually a portal. I asked if this was true, and the word "help" came through.

Cherise: Why are you attached to this doll?

App: Demon.

Cherise: Is the energy around this doll positive or evil?

App: Evil.

I wasn't getting a ton of direct responses to my questions, but a handful of words kept coming through, such as dead, Dave, killed, help, Carol, help me, shut up and shhhh. I closed down the session.

Very early in the morning of the sixth day of having the doll at my house, I thought I heard my son get out of bed and move around the hallway. It sounded like he was creeping down the hall one way and then would creep back the other way. This happened a few times before I got out of bed to see what he was doing, considering it was so early it was still dark out. To my surprise, he was still fast asleep in his bed. My daughter was also in her room, asleep with the door shut, and my husband wasn't home at that time, so it wasn't him. My dog and cat were in bed with me, but clearly *someone* had decided to walk around the hallway that morning. This was interesting to me since the listing had mentioned the doll moving from place to place.

Later that day I conducted my third and final session with the doll. I started with dowsing rods, asking yes and no questions. Throughout my sessions with the doll, I would repeat questions I had already asked before because I was attempting to see if I would get the same answers each time. When I asked if there were multiple spirits attached to the doll, it felt as if the rods were trying to indicate a yes response, but were met with resistance, and I couldn't get an answer. Intuitively it was feeling as if several spirits were trying to communicate with me throughout the week, but one stronger spirit was controlling them or not letting them speak.

Once again I asked if the doll was a portal. The rods indicated a yes answer. I asked if there were both good and bad entities associated with the doll, and the rods indicated yes. I asked if there were any entities that felt stuck or trapped with the doll, and got a yes answer. When I asked if all of the spirits attached to the doll were human, I got a no. I asked if any of the spirits wished to be released from the doll, and got a yes answer. Considering I wasn't entirely sure yet just exactly what it was I was dealing with, I didn't feel comfortable helping to release any spirits connected to the doll.

For the time that the doll had been at my house, I was extra clumsy, tripping over things and dropping things. I didn't sleep well, and my dreams were even more vivid than normal.

My final thoughts on the doll, prior to hearing Amanda's experiences, were that there was absolutely something going on with her. The energy at my home felt off while I had the doll there, and my own energy felt off, as I was finding myself more agitated than normal. This was a little concerning to me considering I had spiritual and magickal safeguards surrounding the doll. To me, this indicated that the energy around the doll is quite strong. I felt as if the doll itself was a type of portal, perhaps with one main guardian spirit running the show.

My week with Betty had come to an end, so Amanda and I conducted a distance Estes session while on video chat. I had the doll placed next to me. I conducted the session using the Necrophonic app, and Amanda used her spirit box. We wanted to try two different devices to see if that impacted the responses at all. We set timers to let us know when our time was up since we weren't in person with one another and wouldn't be able to physically tap each other out of the session. We began with me having headphones on and Amanda asking the questions and then switched to me asking questions while Amanda had headphones on.

BETTY ESTES SESSION

Amanda: Can you say Cherise's name or my name?

Cherise: What's your name?

Amanda: My name's Amanda. Can you say that to Cherise?

Cherise: Yes. Susan.

Amanda: Is your name Susan?

Cherise: Be quiet. (My hands got sweaty.)

Amanda: Are you a human spirit?

Cherise: I'm bad.

Amanda: Do you think you're bad? Do you think you're evil?

Cherise: Spirit. Nothing. Vomit. (I mention how those words each sounded like three different voices.)

Amanda: So I think multiple spirits might be –

Cherise: Betty! (I mention hearing two bells or chime sounds.)

Amanda: Betty, where did you die?

Cherise: Dead.

Amanda: Yes, where did you die?

Cherise: (I heard what sounded like somebody running towards me in the headphones and then a very creepy girl laughing.)

Amanda: I want to know how many spirits are attached to this doll. Can you give me a number?

Cherise: Four? Ew.

Amanda: Are there four of you attached?

Cherise: A lot.

Amanda: Are there human spirits who want help moving on? Do you need help moving on to the next phase?

Cherise. It. Isn't. Possible.

Amanda: Can you try to tap Cherise on the shoulder?

Cherise: (I say that I am starting to feel nauseous.) Nauseous.

Amanda: Are you evil?

Cherise: (Couldn't tell what it said, but it was creepy.) I don't know. Wait, wait, wait. Betsy.

Amanda: Hi, Betsy.

Cherise: Hey.

Amanda: Can you tell Cherise how many fingers I'm holding up? (Proceeds to hold up three fingers to the camera.)

Cherise: Three. Five?

Amanda: (Shocked.) Thank you!

Cherise: Listen.

Amanda: I'm listening.

Cherise: Felt pain. That's it.

Amanda: Why did you feel pain?

Cherise: It was the devil.

Amanda: Can you tell me what year the doll was made? Do one of you know that?

Cherise: ...makes it. But wait. Finish it.

Amanda: Is there something in part of the doll that's making you attracted to it or holding energy? What part of the doll?

Cherise: Neck.

Amanda: Is there something in the neck of the doll?

Cherise: Head. Foot. Head.

Amanda: Is it all over? Is it just the whole doll attracting all this spirit energy?

Cherise: Vessel. Key.

Amanda: Are you glad that we're trying to communicate with you?

Cherise: Pressured.

Amanda: You feel like we're pressuring you?

Cherise: No.

At that point my timer went off, and the session ended. We didn't share with each other the questions and responses, as we didn't want to potentially sway what Amanda would hear in the spirit box or the questions I would ask. We decided to wait until we both had a turn to reveal what came through.

Cherise: To the spirit or energy attached to the doll, are you with Amanda right now?

Amanda: Smoke.

Cherise: She's listening to you, so you can talk to her, and she will repeat what you say. Are you able to do that? To communicate with Amanda, and she will relay the message to me.

Amanda: I'm getting close. (Amanda says she feels like there's someone next to her.)

Cherise: Ok, so you're officially with Amanda, I guess.

Amanda: (Amanda says there's somebody singing in her ear.)

Cherise: Can you tell me your name?

Amanda: (Says she was hearing a female and a male voice.)

Cherise: To the male and female, can you tell me the names?

Amanda: One...two...three...four.

Cherise: So there's four of you there?

Amanda: (Amanda quickly removes the headphones and blindfold to tell me she's weirded out. She says she hears the static like normal, but then almost psychically or somehow outside of the headphones, she hears a woman singing or humming. She composed herself and went back under.)

Cherise: How many spirits are connected to this doll?

Amanda: I'm young. Of course. There's people. Help me.

Cherise: What do you need help with?

Amanda: Some of us. Almost. Who's talking? Shut up. In the room. We're home.

Cherise: Whose home are you at?

Amanda: Please. Do you love me?

Cherise: Can you tell me who was in my hallway?

Amanda: I'm here.

Cherise: Who are you?

Amanda: A different time.

Cherise: Is this doll a spirit magnet?

Amanda: Seven. Thirty. Forty.

Cherise: Do any of you need help?

Amanda: No. No, no, no!

Cherise: Is there a spirit controlling this doll and the energy?

Amanda: How? Eat the body.

Cherise: Is there a spirit controlling this doll and all of the other spirits?

Amanda: I'm outta here.

Cherise: Did I just make you mad?

Amanda: Be careful.

Cherise: Are Amanda and I in danger?

Amanda: I'm haunting this side. Excuse me.

Cherise: Yes?

Amanda. She's dead. Yeah. (Amanda states that it was two voices, one making the statement and another agreeing. She then says she feels like someone is standing in front of her.)

Cherise: Are you standing in front of Amanda?

Amanda: Wait! You asked me what I'm called. It's almost time to go.

Cherise: Do you have anything to say before we go?

Amanda: Yes.

Cherise: What would you like to say before we go?

Amanda: Wait.

Cherise: Wait for what?

Amanda: Quick. (Amanda says she hears a very deep voice but couldn't make out what it was saying.)

Cherise: What do you want to say before we go?

Amanda: I'm scared.

Cherise: I'm sorry, is there a way I can help you?

Amanda's timer goes off, and the session is over.

While Amanda and I had slightly different interactions with the doll during each of our weeks, there were several things that we experienced that were similar, such as I felt irritated every time I would actively investigate her or be around her; Amanda picked up on the irritation from the doll upon opening the package.

We both heard things in the hallway.

My dreams were extra vivid and wild, while Amanda had nightmares.

We both sensed the spirit was not that of an old woman and perhaps could be a trickster-type entity instead or even a portal.

After Amanda and I had concluded each of our weeks with the doll and our final sessions, we held a giveaway for Betty on Instagram, as neither of us wanted to keep her. Unfortunately, this meant that I had to keep Betty at my house for another week or so while we held the contest. The winners of the giveaway ended up being Josh McWilliams and Tamara Cunningham of *Hex-Files* podcast. I happily packaged up Betty and sent her to them down in North Carolina. I was glad that it was Josh and Tamara who won Betty because they have experience in both the paranormal and with witch-craft and magick, so I knew they would be able to handle the doll safely.

Josh and Tamara stated that when Betty arrived to their home, one of their dogs was extremely apprehensive of the doll, and its fur stood up on its back. They too spent some time investigating Betty. They asked Betty, what are you? To which they received an EVP saying "door." The creepy part of that EVP is that the voice sounded eerily similar to Josh's, almost as if the spirit was mimicking his voice. During one of their sessions, they had a thermal camera running. Betty showed up glowing warm on the thermal camera, which theo-retically she shouldn't have, as she's an inanimate object. Tamara sat next to the doll and noted that it felt heavy, like it would if an adult human were sitting next to her. Josh states that other than some weird Estes session responses sometimes, Betty is actually pretty chill. Maybe this is because they didn't immediately place her in a protec-tive bubble like I tried to do, and instead they bring her on some of their haunted excursions and give her attention.

Through the experience with Betty and Josh and Tamara, I now get to call them my friends. Although I'm in Ohio, and they're in North Carolina, we have managed to spend a few weekends together hanging out, investigating and having spooky adventures. On one of these weekends, while staying at an old Victorian home filming a project, they brought Betty along. We wanted to do a video recapping our Betty experiences. This was my first time seeing Betty in person since I had her at my home. Holding her again for the first time in a long while, I still felt the energy connected to her. I was surprised again at the weight to her; she's quite hefty for such a little doll. Josh, Tamara and I were seated in front of the camera, and we had Betty with us. While we were talking, we heard footsteps upstairs, almost as if someone ran back and forth a couple of times. We jokingly looked at Betty, asking if it was her. We didn't think much more of that moment until we all went up to bed.

I was in my room, with Josh and Tamara in the room next to mine. I lay on the bed to relax a little before going to sleep when I noticed that my ceiling fan was changing speed. It would turn off and then on, speed up and then slow down. I grabbed the remote control for the fan and light fixture to try to figure out what was going on, but it didn't seem to be working. I pushed the fan button, but it didn't turn on. I pushed the light button, and it wouldn't turn off. I was starting to get kind of creeped out that it was acting so weird because the remote had been working fine earlier in the day. Tamara then came to my room and asked if perhaps the light switch or something in my room was connected to their ceiling fan and light. I asked her if their light was acting weird as well, and she said it was. I pushed the light button on my remote, and Josh, from the next room, exclaimed that their light just turned on. We realized in that moment that somehow, the remotes for each of our rooms had been switched. And then it hit us all at the same time. The footsteps we'd heard earlier! I absolutely believe that it was Betty playing a trick on us and had run back and forth, switching our room remotes.

It wasn't until writing this book that I made the connection; of course it was Betty! Not only had Amanda heard noises in her hallway when she had Betty at her house, but I also heard her run back and forth in my hallway when I had her, and then she was heard at the house with Josh and Tamara. I'm glad I got to visit with Betty one more time, and it's pretty cool that she's so active, but I'm more glad that she doesn't live with me.

THE HOPE DOLL

In 2020 Steve Hummel, owner of Archive of the Afterlife, was given a doll that he believes is the most haunted doll in his collection. A friend of Steve's came across the doll at an estate sale and immediately felt very uneasy around it. She wanted to give the doll to Steve since he has experience with such items. When Steve first picked up the doll, he got an intuitive impression of child abuse and violence. He thinks this is maybe what created the possibility of a demonic entity being attracted to the doll. People have experienced some pretty scary paranormal activity associated with the doll. It has been said to move on its own, scratch people, make people sick, and even cause bad luck to those who touch it. Investigators who have investigated the doll have had names of demons come through on devices like the spirit box, such as the name Leviathan.

The Hope doll wears a cross around her neck that Steve put on her, and is kept in a case that Steve blessed in order to keep the entity contained. The doll itself is similar in appearance to an American Girl doll, but is taller and not from the same company.

When I visited the Archive of the Afterlife with Sydney Wilson, we were in the Dark Room and investigated the doll. While I was sitting on the opposite side of the room, facing the doll, it looked as if her face was changing expressions slightly. This very well could've been a trick of the dim red lighting on my eyes, but either way it was causing me to feel very uneasy. While the doll itself was staring straight ahead, it felt as though the spirit attached to the doll was the one actually staring at me. And it was annoyed. Earlier in the evening during the tour of the museum that Steve gave us, Sydney asked if she could open the case and touch the doll. Steve told her she could. Could this be why the doll seemed to be irritated? Maybe she didn't like Sydney picking her up out of her case.

Sydney left me alone in the room. While I was introducing myself and talking to the spirit attached to Hope, I saw a small dark orb, several inches off the floor, move from one side of the room to the other.

There was a REM-POD on top of the case the Hope doll sits in. While setting up the equipment, the REM-POD illuminated one time very strongly but was silent and dark after that for the duration of the investigation. We also set an EMF tripwire around the case, which lit up a few times. But other than that, we didn't get much interaction from the Hope doll, unfortunately, even when we tried the spirit box and Estes sessions. This isn't to say that the doll is not haunted or possessed, we just didn't happen to have much activity surrounding her. Enough people have had bizarre and scary encounters with her to lead me to believe that there just might be something attached to her.

MANDY

If you go to the Quesnel Museum and Archives in Canada, you might come across one of their items, an antique doll named Mandy. Mandy was made sometime in the early 1900s and looks innocent enough. She has on a white gown and hat, little white socks and even holds a tiny stuffed lamb toy. But appearances can be deceiving. The doll was donated to the museum in 1991 by a woman who had received the doll from her grandmother when she was little. The doll had been tucked away in a trunk for many years and recently taken out. The donor stated that the doll gave her the creeps, so she wanted to get rid of it.

Shortly after Mandy's arrival to the museum, strange things began to occur. Employees' lunches would go missing, only to be found hours later in a random spot, and other items would go missing. The first night Mandy had been in the museum, she was left in the lab to be photographed the next day. When the employees came back to work, they found the lab in disarray, almost as if a child had thrown a tantrum.[1] That adorable lamb that Mandy holds? It's been found on the floor...next to her *locked* case. Guests to the museum who have tried to take photos or videos of Mandy will either have the images not turn out correctly, or their batteries will die.

While the activity surrounding Mandy can be a little eerie, she doesn't seem to be malicious. Some psychics and sensitives have picked up on the spirit of a little girl attached to Mandy. One who acts a little mischievously whenever she is bored or feeling lonely.

Mandy is still on display at the museum to this day, and you can visit her, if you dare.

RUBY

Ruby, who is in the collection of Greg and Dana Newkirk, owners of Traveling Museum of the Paranormal and Occult, seems to emit a deep sadness. They received the doll from someone who says the doll has been in their family for generations. They believe the doll is haunted by one of their ancestors, a young girl who supposedly died while holding the doll. Whenever people hold Ruby, they are struck by feelings of immense sadness and even nausea. Not only does it seem Ruby has the power to make people feel unwell, but she apparently has the power to move from room to room, being found in one room despite having previously been placed in another.

The Traveling Museum of the Paranormal and Occult frequently brings their items to various conventions and events. If you're lucky, they may travel somewhere near you, and you can have the chance to hold Ruby yourself.

ESMERELDA AT THE VILLA

When I first arrived at McInteer Villa with the crew to film the documentary, we got a tour from Stephanie, the home's owner. While on the tour, we made notes of things we might be feeling in certain rooms so as to refer to it later during our investigation. I felt various vibes throughout the home, but the energy seemed different as we entered one of the bedrooms, which people call the Doll Room or the Kids' Room. This room is furnished with two beds, a love seat, some dressers, and dolls. Lots of dolls. Several of the dolls gave me an uneasy feeling, but it was one in particular that both myself and fellow investigator Nat immediately felt nervous about. Stephanie informed us that the doll's name is Esmerelda. Esmerelda is an antique marionette doll, made with real human hair, and she is housed in a mirror-lined wooden case. Stephanie wasn't sure of the history of the doll but stated that the doll sometimes makes people uncomfortable. She certainly was making me feel uncomfortable. While, yes, the doll is visually a little unsettling, it's the energy it emits that made me the most uneasy.

During our two-day, two-night investigation of the villa, it seemed that things kept coming back to Esmerelda. Responses we received on the spirit box that seemed to imply Esmerelda was causing activity, the EMF meter lighting up near her case, and even a camera falling over near her case. For me, the most frightening moment that possibly involved Esmerelda was on our last night of the investigation. It was the middle of the night, and we had finished filming. Our director and Eliot were downstairs putting gear away. Nat and I were in the upstairs hallway, with the doll room at the far end. I'm not sure who noticed it first, but we saw a tall shadow figure leaning out from the stairs next to the Doll Room. We watched as the figure would sort of sway, leaning in and out. Excitedly, we yelled for the guys to come upstairs with a camera. They got to the top of the stairs, and as Nat and I were telling them to look down the hall to see if they noticed the figure, our director pointed at the window in the doll room, above Esmerelda's case.

"What *is* that!?" he said.

All of our eyes looked up towards the window within the darkened room. Outside the window was a bright flashing white light. It wasn't a plane or lightning, and the best way I can describe it was almost like a strobe light being shone through the windowpanes. As we stared at this light flashing and illuminating the doll room, we saw the shadow figure again. Suddenly, the entire energy of the house shifted. The amount of fear that washed over us was intense, and at that moment we all took off running down the stairs. Now, as an experienced spiritual practitioner and paranormal investigator, I'm not proud to say I ran. But I have never felt that type of paranormal fear and panic before in my life. I truly think that what we were encountering was something not of this plane of existence and something that's quite dark and powerful.

After investigating at McInteer Villa and having our experiences with Esmerelda, I was curious to know more about her origins, so I took to the internet. Esmerelda appeared to be a puppet from an Asian country, so that was what I searched for: antique marionettes from Asia. It wasn't long before I spotted images of other puppets that were quite similar to Esmerelda. I quickly learned that she is a type of puppet from Myanmar (formerly Burma). These intricate marionettes are called yoke thé and are part of a set of twenty-eight puppets operated by skilled puppeteers that tell a detailed story. When reading about these puppets, something that stood out to me was the concept that the puppeteers consider these marionettes as living beings with spirits of their own. Prior to a performance, an offering is made, and the puppets are "brought to life."[2]

I wanted to know more about these marionettes, and specifically Esmerelda, so I reached out to a puppet museum. Portland Puppet Museum director and Olde World Puppet Theater creator Steve Overton shared some great information with me in regard to these Myanmar marionettes. Steve told me that the marionettes have been around for roughly eight hundred years, and the shows were originally performed for royalty before eventually being performed for the "common folk." A unique feature for these particular puppets is that they are all anatomically correct, which Steve says is rare in the puppet world. Each puppet is hand carved, and the creator will rub their spit and blood into the puppet, essentially putting a piece of them into the marionette with the idea that a part of their spirit will live forever within the puppet. It's also not uncommon for the dolls to be made with human hair, which Esmerelda has. Steve says these puppets can act as a sort of battery, holding onto the energy of the original creator as well as any other puppeteers or those who have enjoyed the performances. He believes a spirit might attach to the marionette because of the close relationship the puppeteer and puppet have. I showed him a photo of Esmerelda, and he told me that it is the character of the Prince, and that it is a professional puppet more than eighty years old.

The Portland Puppet Museum has many beautiful and intricate Myanmar marionettes, but Steve says none of them have given him a creepy feeling; however, a man brought in his own marionette one time that gave Steve a very bad vibe, and he told the man to put salt on the puppet when he got home. While none of the puppets at the museum bring about a creepy feeling, that's not to say that they aren't a little mischievous. Steve told me they like to hide sometimes. He was setting up an exhibit only to find that two of the marionette crates were missing, only to show up randomly later, and that other items move or seemingly disappear at the museum. One time, an EVP was captured at the museum, clearly stating, "I am alive." He says he believes the puppets don't mean any harm, but they do want attention.

Considering how marionettes like Esmerelda are created, paired with the love and attention the puppeteers place on them, it's not surprising to think that one could be haunted with a spirit. Why this particular spirit attached to Esmerelda seems angry remains a mystery. However, the idea of vengeful spirits in Myanmar could be an indicator.

While doing research on the marionettes of Myanmar, I came across the topic of Nats. Nat spirits are considered spirits of those who died violent or traumatic deaths. Despite this, they can be seen as protectors of forests, villages, and people's health or well-being.[3] When pleased, the Nat spirits can bestow blessings upon the people; however, if they are displeased, they are known to cause havoc and misery. The belief in Nats predates Buddhism as the main religion in the region. Despite Buddhism being practiced by the majority of those in Myanmar, folk beliefs and traditions still run strong. It's not uncommon to see Nat statues throughout the cities and villages, or even in people's homes. It's thought that these statues, as well as festivals and offerings, help to appease the Nat spirits. Could Esmerelda be haunted or possessed by one of these Nat spirits? Angry and vengeful to not be receiving the praise and recognition it desires? While investigating the McInteer Villa, we heard the word "Nat" come through the spirit box multiple times. During the moment, we assumed the spirit was calling out Nat's name, one of the investigators. However, with the research I have done, I wonder if, instead, we were being told the type of spirit that we were communicating with. It could have been the spirit trying to tell us who it was and, therefore, what it needed and wanted.

While researching the Nat spirits, I came across the topic of Nat-Kadaws. Nat-Kadaws are a type of shaman and are seen as spirit mediums for the Nat spirits. During Nat festivals (Nat-Pwe), they can become possessed by these spirits to deliver messages and healings to the people. Through offerings and praise, the Nats may choose to offer blessings. This is done through Nat festivals or privately sponsored smaller ceremonies.[4] Sometimes, the Nat-Kadaw may become tormented by one of the spirits and must "marry" it in order to appease the spirit and find peace once more. This is done through a ceremony in which the soul is trapped in a mirror, and the Nat spirit takes its place. I find this extremely interesting in regard to Esmerelda considering all of the mirror connections we had during our investigation. During my research, I found no direct connection between the Nats, Nat-Kadaw and the marionettes. I asked Steve at the Portland Puppet Museum if he had heard of any connection between the marionettes and the Nats, but he wasn't aware of any. He imagines it is possible though, especially if the puppet was in one of the temples or someone died not long after puppeteering it. I do find it intriguing that the same country that created the puppet that now resides at the villa also has a ritual of trapping a soul in a mirror. I do believe there is enough of a correlation here to warrant looking more deeply into this. I'm hoping one day to be able to return to the McInteer Villa, armed with this information, to specifically investigate Esmerelda.

I asked Nat if she wanted to share her perspective of our investigation and experiences with Esmerelda, and she emailed me the following:

When we first arrived at the McInteer Villa, it seemed very welcoming. Beautiful antique furniture, and the whole place fully refurbished. It was like walking into a Victorian time capsule. My mind was quickly changed as we started our tour. There were, of course, your average ghosts at this location, no doubt about that, but after what we experienced, we came to the conclusion there was something else, something darker.

When we approached the second floor, something or someone was making itself known from the room all the way at the end. I poked Eliot, my partner, and pointed to the area that felt off. I was trying my hardest not to interrupt the tour that was being given. When we approached the room, of course it had to be the doll room, filled with many dolls. Not just your ordinary dolls, some had no bodies, some were from other haunted locations, but there was one that really stood out more than the others. The feeling it gave off was as it if were very much alive, as if another person were in the room, watching us take this tour. I turned to the owner, Stephanie, and pointed to the doll, who was named Esmeralda. I said quietly, "That one." The owner looked at me and said that I was the third psychic to have said that.

After our first night there investigating, it was time to pick where we were going to sleep. Eliot gladly volunteered for the doll room. I don't think any of us slept through the whole night without some sort of strange disturbance. The next morning Eliot mentioned his strange disturbance, that he'd heard little doll-like feet moving around as he tried to sleep. We decided to go back into the doll room to see if we could try to figure out what was the noise that Eliot had heard. Could these doll feet be debunked? Possibly, though we could not find an actual source. As we were about to leave the room, I noticed that it looked like Esmeralda had moved just slightly from the previous day. I asked Eliot, could it have possibly been the feet of an old marionette puppet?

He responded, "Actually...yeah." We both gazed over at Esmeralda, then slowly left the room.

We knew the owner was coming back later that day, and I wanted to take advantage of really knowing what this doll was about. She did not know much about Ezzie, this was the doll's nickname, other than the fact that the doll's hair is real human hair. Since we had a good feel of the location, we were curious what sort of evidence had been captured there, to compare it with what we were dealing with during the first night. Stephanie started showing us some amazing EVPs and visual evidence. Some things that we noticed during this showing were full-body apparitions that were caught in the doll room, along with very vulgar EVPs right above Ezzie, where a security camera had been placed. There was also a photo of a picture of a man with dark hair and a pale face, that was captured in the downstairs dining room mirror, that had no logical explanation. Oddly enough, the pale face and dark hair were both characteristics that Ezzie also had. Little did we know this picture of the man in the mirror had a huge tie to the second night that we were about to experience.

The second night at the villa was much more active than the first. We started to notice strange little black shadows hopping from one room to the next. During this night, we decided to spend some time in the mirror room. This was literally a closet room surrounded with mirrors. This was the first time in my life I ever tried scrying. Since this night, I have purchased my own scrying mirror to practice a bit, because after this experience, I wouldn't recommend anyone who hasn't tried scrying to do it at this location. From my own personal view, I definitely felt like this was when the energy became downright creepy. When it was Eliot's turn to do the scrying, he saw a pale like figure go past, not the mirror he was scrying in, but the one next to it.

Later in the night, Cherise was looking for silverware; she discovered a polaroid of an old mirror in one of the drawers, which was a very strange place for a picture to be, especially a photo of a single mirror.

As we investigated room to room, we started to notice that every single room had a mirror. Then something clicked. I immediately ran upstairs. The only doll that had its own case that involved a mirror was, of course, Esmeralda. I looked at the doll and asked if it was her, as if we just put the last piece of the puzzle together. When we turned around, there was a painting on the wall of a girl looking in a mirror.

The links between the mirrors at this point were very unsettling, and very convincing there was a connection. That night we all decided to sleep on the couches downstairs, because at this point, we were unsure what exactly it was we were dealing with. Mirror portals are something I personally hadn't explored too much into at the time, but I had a feeling whatever was attached to Ezzie was using these mirrors to hop from room to room. This would also help explain the shadow darting across the room, then disappearing into the other.

Now, if you are a paranormal investigator, depending on where you are sleeping, a face mask and earplugs are a must-have. I am a very light sleeper; in order to get any rest, without these items I personally cannot sleep at all. The night we slept on the couches, I was woken up by this entity. Sitting myself up while reaching to take off my face mask, something hissed in my face. At that point, I threw off my face mask just in time to see the little black shadow dart into the next room, right into the mirror. That is one way to say good morning.

After our experience with Esmeralda and the McInteer Villa, I started researching more on where Ezzie possibly came from. While researching, I stumbled upon Asian marionette puppets that looked very similar to her. These puppets were made from real human hair and could have been passed down throughout centuries. On the topic of Asian culture, I also discovered mirror people. In Chinese folklore, the mirror people emerge from their reflective surfaces and can enter our world from a gateway of a parallel world. In legend, they were afflicted with a spell that bound them to the mirror world, where they are now cursed to mimic every move of their human counterparts, whenever those look at a reflective surface. Could Esmeralda possibly be a mirror person? Or someone who was once living, and parts of their self are still attached to this doll? This all still remains a mystery.

It's hard to truly convey the energy and things we were feeling during our time at the McInteer Villa and our interactions with Esmerelda. But this was one of the most eerie and unsettling investigations I've ever been on in my life. Proof that even though a home might be beautiful, it can also hold a darkness to it. That being said, not all of the spirits that reside there are dark or sinister. It's quite the opposite. There is a friendliness and love throughout the home, in part from the spirits there and in part due to the attention Stephanie brings to the villa. If you ever find yourself at the 1889 McInteer Villa, perhaps just steer clear of the mirrors...and Esmerelda.

CHARLEY THE DOLL

Charley the haunted doll is one of those dolls that just *looks* haunted. He's old, and he's creepy. Half the paint is rubbed off his face, and he looks like he's been through some stuff. People aren't quite sure how old the doll actually is, but he was found in 1968 in a trunk in the attic of a Victorian home. The only things in the trunk besides the doll were old newspapers from the 1930s and a withered paper that had the Lord's Prayer written on it.[5] The family who found the doll already had a collection of older dolls, so they placed the doll (that they named Charley) amongst the rest of their collection. Nothing seemed amiss; however, soon the family noticed that Charley would be in different places on the doll bench than he had previously been left. The parents assumed one of their five children were moving the doll even though the kids all claimed to not move him. Then one day, their youngest daughter said that the doll had spoken to her the night before. The children became increasingly more and more unsettled by the doll, with one of the children even waking up with scratches all over their body. It was at this point the parents locked the doll back into the trunk in the attic. Activity seemed to cease.

There in the dark trunk Charley stayed until years later when the children were all grown and sold the home. The trunk itself was one of the last items to be sold from the home, to a woman. The woman claimed to feel uneasy around the doll and noticed him being in places that he previously wasn't. She never heard him speak or received mysterious scratches on her body. Charley seems to reserve that for children.

After having been passed to several different owners, Charley the Doll now resides in a shop called Local Artisan, located in Massachusetts. If you find yourself in the area, pop into the shop and give ol' Charley a hello.

ISLAND OF THE DOLLS

When I first heard there was a haunted island with dolls all over it, I was immediately intrigued, and it has remained on my bucket list to this day. South of Mexico City you will find Isla de la Muñecas, or Island of the Dolls. While the island itself has grown in notoriety and is on many people's travel lists, it began as a tribute to a young girl who died too soon, and wasn't created with the intention of it being a travel destination.

Years ago there was a caretaker named Don Julian Santana Barrera, who lived on the island. One day, he found the body of a little girl in the canal who had washed up ashore. Not long after pulling her body from the water and attempting to save her (to no avail), a doll floated down the water to the island. To appease the girl's spirit, and in honor of her, he hung the doll that he presumed to be hers from a tree branch. But apparently this wasn't enough. He claimed to be haunted by her spirit, so he began to bring more and more dolls to the island in hopes of keeping her spirit happy. However, he eventually realized that the dolls were becoming inhabited by the spirits of other dead children. Some wonder if the story was true or not, and if it was, perhaps Julian was never able to heal his guilt of not being able to save the girl. And it was this guilt that caused him to believe the dolls were haunted. Sadly, some fifty years and many, many, dolls later, Don Julian was found dead on the island, in roughly the same spot he claimed the little girl had died. After Julian passed away in 2001, more and more tourists have gone to the island. Always making sure to bring a doll to appease the spirits.

Visitors to the island have claimed to hear voices and even capture the dolls moving in photos and video. While Don Julian's actions of bringing the dolls to the island was done out of compassion, it's hard to ignore the eerie visuals of weathered dolls hanging from trees. And the energy surrounding them, as well as the island, continues to give people the creeps even today.

Chapter Four

HAUNTED FURNITURE

SARAH'S HAUNTED ROCKING CHAIR

I once got a chair from an antique shop. I put it in the corner of my bedroom and had planned for it to be my nursing chair for my second child. Every night I would wake up and see a woman in a dress, like an early schoolhouse teacher dress, sitting in it. I asked her to leave again and again, but I kept seeing her in it at night. She wouldn't leave, so eventually I put the chair on the curb with a note that it came with a ghost and to take with caution...and someone took it! Never saw the woman again after that. I don't even think I asked the ghost woman what her deal was, I was too annoyed, haha.

– Submitted by Sarah Petruno

Sarah's story makes me wonder if the chair was haunted residually or intelligently. It doesn't seem the ghost woman that Sarah saw said anything or interacted with her, which makes me think that it was more of an energetic imprint on the chair. Perhaps this was a chair that the woman had sat in night after night while she was alive, which left her spiritual imprint upon it. Curious to know who picked up the chair off the curb and if they're having any experiences or if it was Sarah's intuition that allowed her to see this spiritual imprint. Would you pick up a piece of furniture from the side of the road that potentially came with a ghost included?

THE ANTIQUE OWNER'S BED SET

While I was perusing my neighborhood antique store the other day, one of the booth owners happened to be there stocking her section with some new items. Considering antique stores are known to house all sorts of objects with various histories and hauntings, I asked her if she happened to have any experiences of the paranormal kind. She told me she did, but requested to remain anonymous. This is her story:

I have been doing this for about thirty years. Picking great antique finds. That's how I furnish my house, and I also sell them in my booth. And so the one haunted object that I did find, unfortunately, was a bedroom set, the whole set, and it carried a whole lot of energy. The first night that I slept in it, I had my first instance of sleep paralysis ever. And my husband had a string of protection beads that he made me, and I hung them on the bedpost that night. The next morning the string had broken. That was my first and last night in that bed. It was out at the curb the next day, and the neighbors were looking at me, and I'm like "this is really not a curb pick that you want to pick up."

I do believe that energy, that lots of things carry energy, and so a lot of the times you can feel it. Especially when you go into an estate sale, you might feel the leftover energy that's still kind of zooming around.

I did go into an estate sale that was a former chapel for various reli-
gions, and I did not end up buying a lot of stuff from that. They did
have several Buddhist items, which I did buy a couple. I felt they had
really good energy. But there were a lot of dolls, and I find that
fabric retains more energy than almost anything else. So I'm very
careful about fabric. There are several things I always buy new, like a
new mattress 'cause I'm not sleeping on someone else's. And I think
we also give so much of our energy away when we're sleeping and rest-
ing, for something like a mattress to absorb.

The antique dealer brings up an interesting point regarding fabrics
retaining more energy than other materials. Does the density of an
object contribute to the amount of energy it is capable of absorbing?
I would be curious to study that theory more deeply; however, it
seems that regardless of the material an item is made with, there is
always a chance for it to become haunted.

BUSBY'S STOOP CHAIR

Thomas Busby was to be executed, but not before creating a curse. In
1702 in North Yorkshire, United Kingdom, Busby was to be
executed by hanging for the murder of his father-in-law, Daniel Auty.
Auty and Busby ran a coin-counterfeiting business together, and it's
said that their argument stemmed over Busby's treatment of his wife,
Auty's daughter. Whatever the reason, Busby was arrested, charged,
and executed. At the crossroads where his body hung (and by some
accounts was left to hang long after his death) sat an inn. One version
of the story states that it was at this very inn that Busby was at when
he got arrested. Another version states that on his way to be executed,
he asked for one final drink, which was had at the inn. Regardless of
which story is true, his ghost supposedly haunts the inn to this day.
Busby was no stranger to this particular inn, as he had his own chair

that he always sat in while having drinks. The legend says that whether it was when he got arrested or while having his final drink, he cursed the chair, saying, "May sudden death come to anyone who dare sit in my chair." And if the stories are true, the curse worked.

In the late 1800s a chimney sweep was brave enough, or fool enough, to sit in the chair. The next morning, he was found hanging dead outside the inn. During World War 2, Canadian soldiers dared each other to sit in the chair. They never returned after being sent off on a mission. Even more deaths surrounded the chair and those who sat in it, including people who fell over dead days later or even got in fatal car accidents leaving the inn. The chair had called the Busby Stoop Inn its home, but in the late 1970s was moved to the Thirsk Museum, where it now resides...hanging from the ceiling to prevent anyone from sitting on it.

According to some researchers, there is no way the story of the haunted chair is real due to the fact that it appears the chair would have been made in the decades following the execution of Busby. If the curse of Busby isn't real, then what could be causing the apparent deaths associated with the chair? Is it superstition getting the better of people or something else?

THE TALLMAN BUNK BEDS

The year is 1987, and the Tallman family is living in Wisconsin. Debbie and Allen purchased a bunk bed for their children from a secondhand shop. They say when they brought the bed home, paranormal activity happened almost immediately. They would hear disembodied voices, doors opening and shutting on their own, and the radio turning on by itself. The kids claimed to see a woman with long dark hair in their bedroom. The activity was so intense that the family had their pastor come in to bless the home. Things seemed to only increase to horrifying levels when Allen heard a voice from the garage telling him to "come here." When he went to look in the garage, he saw that it was illuminated with a glowing orange light with red eyes staring back at him. The case began to garner so much attention that it was even featured on the show *Unsolved Mysteries* in 1988. Eventually the Tallmans were able to trace the beginning of the paranormal activity to the bunk beds. They destroyed the bed and threw it in a landfill. Activity ceased.

THE CONSTRUCTION VANITY

The following story was submitted to me by an individual who wishes to remain anonymous.

In the 1980s, I was helping to take down an old hewn lumber house, which still had antique furniture in it. There was a big vanity, a heavy one, which was in a bedroom that we had to move it out of. The problem was, the door was too small for the vanity. We wondered how they got it in there; one of our group suggested that they built the house around it. It had a huge mirror, which was beveled around the edges, and I think the reflector in the glass was some kind of metal, perhaps even mercury, which was used in making mirrors in the early 1800s. So I said to the guys, hang on a minute, and let me check something out. We had pulled it away from the wall, swept the spiderwebs away, and I took a flashlight and looked behind it and under it. It had been assembled with screws. I had come across problems like this before and then had taken the vanity apart and got it out that way. So I said I'd take it apart while other guys began working on other parts of the house, getting the good wood and usable items from the house for reuse.

So I began taking the vanity apart and had to use a torque wrench with the screwdriver to loosen the screws they were in there so tight. While doing this, and the other guys were in a different part of the house, I began to hear what sounded like a woman humming. We were the only ones in the house, and the guys were in another room; no one else was there. I stood up and looked around the bedroom; no one was to be seen. I shrugged and went back to work, and the humming started again. I got back up and figured the guys were playing a joke on me, and I went back out into the room there were in and asked them if they were trying to spook me, and they said no. I asked them to come in and listen to the humming I was hearing. They came in, and of course, nothing happened while they were there. So they went back to the other room and went back to work.

Nothing happened for a bit until I got the mirror frame part loose and was taking it off, and I heard a sharp "OH" and almost dropped the mirror. I set it down on the floor and leaned it against the wall. By now, I was beginning to think that somehow, whoever was humming, their essence was in that vanity. I took the rest of the vanity apart, and the guys loaded it into their truck, one of their relatives wanted it, and I was glad to see it gone. Nothing more happened after that in the house, which was taken down, and the scraps burned.

Chapter Five

HAUNTED PAINTINGS

WHEN IT COMES to haunted paintings, I often wonder if the painting itself is legitimately haunted or if the imagery of the painting stirs something within the viewer, making them uncomfortable, which causes them to believe the painting is haunted. If someone truly believes something is haunted, then it will be easy for them to attribute any odd happenings or emotions to the "ghost" or "curse" of the artwork. Similarly, when someone believes something to be haunted, there is the theory that they might actually be able to create a type of haunting. Almost like creating a thought form or, at the very least, feeding their frightened energy onto the painting, which other people might be able to pick up on, consequently fueling the haunted theory.

There is another theory that things a person creates, like artwork, become a reflection of what they were feeling at that moment. And that others can feel that when coming into contact with the artwork. For example, if someone was feeling particularly joyful, viewers of the painting might feel uplifted when looking at it. Alternatively, if the artist was feeling anguish, sorrow or hatred while painting, perhaps that energy gets leaked into the painting, causing viewers of the art to feel on edge and uncomfortable. It's perhaps these strong emotions that lead some spirits to haunt various paintings, as they feel attracted to the energy.

THE HANDS RESIST HIM

A painting so hauntingly eerie that people who simply view prints of it have paranormal experiences. This painting is of a young boy and a doll standing in front of a glass door with tiny hands pressed against the glass from the inside. The painting is from the 1970s, titled *The Hands Resist Him,* by Williams Stoneham. It is based on a photo of himself as a five-year old child. In regard to the painting, the artist on his website states:[1] There are memories, echoes of all the life within a place. The hands are "the other lives." The glass door, that thin veil between waking and dreaming. The girl/doll is the imagined companion, or guide through this realm.

In 1974 the painting was in a gallery show led by Charles Feingarten. The painting sold to actor John Marley, and the *Los Angeles Times* art critic Henry Seldis wrote an article on the painting. Ten years later all three of these men would be dead. Marley died in 1984 and had sold the painting prior to his death. To whom? Nobody is quite sure. However, the painting was discovered years later in a California art space. A year later the owners, who wanted to remain anonymous, listed it on eBay. The owners of the painting stated that they really loved the painting and, at first, couldn't figure out why someone would discard it. That is, until their young daughter told them that the children in the painting would fight and come out of the painting at night. They claimed to have set up a motion camera one night to see if they could capture the painting coming to life, and supposedly they did. That is when they decided to get rid of it and put it up for auction on the website.

Apparently this painting was so haunted that people who merely saw photos of it online had experiences. Some people claimed to have felt faint or sick while looking at the painting, and someone even claimed to have heard a demonic voice while viewing the image. Almost everyone who looks at this painting agrees that it is quite unsettling.

Gallery owner Kim Smith won the eBay auction of the painting and keeps it locked away in a back room. Smith has no plans on selling the painting.

THE ANGUISHED MAN

Sean Robinson inherited a painting. But it's not any old painting. This one is haunted as hell. Robinson inherited the painting from his grandmother, and he says she told him the artist is unknown. However, the artist mixed his own blood into the paint and died by suicide shortly after completing it. How his grandmother knows those facts but not who actually created the painting is definitely something to consider. However, Robinson says the painting is haunted. He claims to have heard moaning in his home where the painting hung, footsteps and banging. He has seen the apparition of a man in his home when the painting is there. The painting has supposedly caused extreme nausea and even nosebleeds for those in its presence.

If the painting was in fact done by the artist mixing their own blood into the paint, this could certainly contribute to unique energy surrounding the painting. However, I would like to think that people are simply creeped out by the imagery itself and that some poor tortured soul isn't stuck within the canvas.

AMANDA'S HAUNTED PAINTING

Amanda Paulson acquired a very creepy-looking painting from a thrift store. The painting is of a man on a canvas, in various shades of green paint. The current painting has been done on top of the original painting. The majority of the painting and the man are done in dark green shades with lots of shadows. However, the most striking and honestly terrifying part of the painting is the man's eyes. His eyes are a very light green and are simultaneously lifeless *and* piercing, contrasting against the deep hues of the rest of the painting. While video chatting with Amanda, I asked her to share the story of how she came across the painting as well as the activity she has experienced since having it in her possession.

So I bought this painting at Value Village, which is a thrift store. For I think $2.99, which is significantly cheaper than a lot of paintings there normally. So that caught my attention. It's also very jarring looking; the eyes caught my attention. I bought it because it was creepy, and I wanted something creepy. I'm fine with that. But I didn't necessarily think it was haunted right away. And I didn't have any activity happen for a couple of weeks until I went out of town. It was the first time I had been out of town since I bought the painting. And then when I came home, Nate (her boyfriend) told me that he had heard some weird sounds in the apartment, like somebody walking around. And then we had something fall off the wall in our kitchen

that's been there forever, and then one of the lightbulbs in our hallway went out, which has also never gone out before. So that was kind of the start of the activity, and then I started feeling like somebody was in my office where the painting is. So I gave it a bowl of water as an offering and made a deal with it and said, "If you keep the activity to a minimum and don't freak me out, then you're allowed to stay." And I hadn't had any activity again since I gave it the water, until the new moon a couple of weeks ago, which is actually interesting timing.

On the new moon I was lighting some candles with my back turned to the painting, and I felt somebody run up or rush up behind me. That's really interesting because most of the time any activity stays outside this room, and I feel like it's in another room, watching me, and never interrupts what I'm doing. But this was different; this came right up to me. So I stopped, and I tried to make a video about it, but as I was trying to talk about it on video, energy kept kicking up, and I would feel someone walking up or walking around. Like right in front of the painting. So I gave up trying to record. But that's the last time something happened. I tried to film a video about it again a couple of nights ago, and it's been really difficult and really weird. Like every time I try to make a video about it, something happens.

As for the history of the painting, there is some writing on the back of the canvas. It tells us the artist of the first painting, which is Landscape by Highway *by a guy named Reese Court, and he's from the area (Spokane, Washington). Likely still alive today, so I think the original painting was done probably around the 1970s, based on the frame. But the top painting we have no information on. The way it's painted is just so strange. It's like, why would somebody paint like that? It's painted in black and a green, like a light green over the black. So it has a really weird effect. And he has eyeglasses on, but they didn't use lighter paint to make them, they just piled up the black paint to make it textured.*

There's no signature on the front or anything. The guy is standing in front of something, like windows or a staircase or something.

When I first got it, I did try to do a (psychic) reading on it, and I saw a lighthouse. I saw an institutionalized woman, very angry. I got the feeling that whoever she was painting she had an affinity for. Like she loved him or cared about him, I don't know. But overall the feeling was that the person painting it was very angry but that the person who was painted was not angry; he was fine. I feel like the energy attached to the painting is an amalgamation of the person who was painted and the person who painted it, like the feelings of it all. I don't know, it was weird.

But then also, I was doing a reading for somebody else, and in my reading I was seeing the person getting her hair washed at a salon. The salon had all glass windows and a glass door. I looked out the window, and I saw a short [man], maybe five-foot-tall, all black-charred or burned face with just eyeballs, no eyelids or eyelashes. And he was pacing outside peering in; it was so scary. He's just looking in, staring, so I walk over to him. At first I walked over to him, thinking I was going to mentally let him in. But then I realized there was something weird about it, so we just came face-to-face up against this window, and he just stood there and stared up at me. I got so freaked out I utilized the white light visualization tactic because I was so overwhelmed by it. I basically disintegrated the entire vision and ended the session. I was just sitting there like, oh my gosh, that just happened. It felt so real and out of my control. In hindsight, he technically didn't do anything wrong; he was just very unnerving. So I have some reservations about him.

THE CRYING BOY

A sad and forlorn-looking young boy with tears pouring from his sad eyes is a famous painting by artist Giovanni Bragolin (whose real name was Bruno Amadio) and is one of a series of paintings from the 1950s. Many prints were made of this painting and hung in many people's homes. Why so many people wanted a painting of a sad little boy, I don't know. Fast-forward to the 1980s, and a UK magazine, *The Sun,* published an article about the supposed curse of this particular painting. A married couple had suffered a severe fire in their home that started in the kitchen. The only thing to not be destroyed by soot and flames? *The Crying Boy* painting hanging in their living room. They claim it must have been the painting itself to cause the fire. After this article was released, a fireman claimed to have been to over a dozen home fires, all of which were destroyed except for one thing...*The Crying Boy* painting. More and more stories began to circulate, all claiming that house fires were caused by having the painting hanging in their home.

The stories snowballed so much that it seemed that any house fire that occurred where there was a painting of *any* crying child (again, why this type of art was so popular, I don't know) it was because of *The Crying Boy.* People began to speculate why the painting was cursed, making up stories about the little boy. They said he was an orphan whose parents were killed in a fire, that he accidentally set fire to the artist's studio when he was being painted, or even that his parents hated the artist and put a curse on him.

Fire marshals tried to state that all of the fires were caused by human error or other explainable causes; however, they weren't able to explain so easily why the painting would often be the only thing left undamaged. Theories are that the prints of the painting had been done with some type of ink or varnish that helped make it more flame resistant.

Whether the painting is actually cursed or not, I won't be hanging it in my home any time soon.

THE HAUNTED GIRL

If you visit the Driskill Hotel in Austin, Texas, you will see the painting of a little girl holding flowers. But this isn't any old painting, it's haunted. The legend states that in the 1880s, the four-year-old daughter, Samantha, of US Senator Temple Lea Houston died tragically at the hotel by tripping and falling down the main staircase in the hotel. It wasn't long after her death that people claimed to see her ghost in the hallways, bouncing a ball and giggling. The story continues to say that her father commissioned artist Richard King to paint a portrait of his daughter to hang in the hotel. Apparently, it was at this point that her spirit decided to enter the painting. It's said that if you stare at the painting long enough, her expression will change. Some even say they feel sick to their stomach or even have the sensation of levitating. There's only a couple of problems with this story. Firstly, the girl in the painting is not Samantha Houston. The painting is in fact done by Richard King; however, it is titled *Love Letters* and was a replication of an older painting by Charles Garland. And secondly, it appears that the senator didn't have a daughter named Samantha; however, he did have a son named Sam.

Even though some of the key facts to this haunting story don't line up, it doesn't mean that the painting isn't actually haunted, or that the ghost of a little girl isn't seen throughout the hotel. With so many people claiming to have experiences with her ghost, it would lead one to believe that there is in fact something eerie going on at the Driskill.

Chapter Six

MISCELLANEOUS HAUNTED OBJECTS

THE DREADFUL PENNY

Sometimes, creepy encounters with objects don't occur due to a specific object being haunted. But rather, objects that seem to materialize out of paranormal origins. The following story was submitted by my friend Vanessa and is an eerie account of such a thing.

I will begin this bizarre, dreadful yet somewhat humorous anecdote by sharing an unusual fact about myself – I've had a phobia of pennies for as long as I can remember, an aversion to anything copper, really. The smell alone is revolting, and I especially could not lay eyes on the dirtier, blackened ones found on sidewalks or between crumby car seats. Ironically, my part-time job as a teen was a cashier at a grocery store, where I had to handle change during cash transactions. I cringed every single time a customer poured sweaty coins into my hand, or I had to scoop a penny from the till, which was done ever so swiftly, mitigating the length of time it was in contact with my skin. Sometimes I told customers not to worry about giving me the three cents change even if that meant my till was short for the night, and other times, I lied and said I ran out of penny change just to avoid yet another stomach-turning encounter. I still cringe thinking about it. Did I ever keep a change jar at home? Absolutely not! Pennies did not reside in my wallet, in my room, nor anywhere near me because I didn't accept them when making purchases. They were basically banned from my life outside of work. But of course, as a teen, off-beat quirks are sure to be discovered, highlighted and poked fun at.

One Friday night at a friend's house, that's exactly what happened. My friends learned of my phobia and decided it would be hilarious to toss pennies at me and watch me crawl right out of my skin! While I squirmed about, trying to avoid getting hit, they laughed and got a rise from my reactions and discomfort around what is basically a harmless, mundane object. My family also knew and never pushed my boundaries, but I gave a little more leeway to friends. Personally, I would've preferred other means of entertainment, but all in all, it was simply just innocent teasing between kids.

But little did I know, it wasn't humans and pennies I had to be wary of...

The unseen or spirit world is real, it exists, and just like any other realm, you will find it inhabited by a full spectrum of beings – loved ones who have passed on, to more mischievousness, ill-intentioned ghosts and everything in between. Earthbound ghosts can be drawn to us for specific reasons we may not be aware of, to simply observe, listen and enjoy our energy. Some darker entities; however, will even collect information on us to play on our fears when least expected. And this is where my tale takes a turn.

The very next Friday night, it was late and time to wind down. I put on pajamas and started my bathroom routine just before bed. I had washed my face, brushed my teeth, and the next task was a final inspec-

tion of my skin. *A few seconds after bending over and leaning on the counter to look in the mirror – I felt what could only be described as cold fingers slowly running down my spine. A chill ran through my entire body; my eyes grew wide; I shot straight up! This sensation was so foreign, so out of the blue and unnerving, I nearly jumped out of my skin. My body shivered again as if to get this icky feeling off, and as I readjusted and smoothed out my T-shirt – a penny fell off my back, dropping and clinking on the cold hard tiles before rolling to a stop.*

Frozen in disbelief, my brain attempted to piece together what just occurred, but none of it made any logical sense. Creepy cold touch. Materialization of a physical object out of thin air – but not any old object – a penny, to boot! I let out a scream so loud it probably woke up the entire neighborhood.

My uncle came rushing to my rescue, thinking who knows what! After all, it was his house we lived in temporarily as ours was being built. It was his house, where many more ghostly encounters would begin for me. This was just the start. Visibly shaken, I still recounted every detail. He tried to calm me down, then noticed the penny on the floor. To my utter shock, he picked it up, held it in his hands and closed his eyes. What on earth was he doing?! A moment later he opened his eyes and, with slight seriousness and curiosity, said, "They're just messing with you..." Stunned. Shocked. Scared to death. I got a flashback of the previous Friday with my friends – it finally started making sense. It's as if the entity that existed in our home recognized my fear and knew it could gain an even greater rise out of me through much more menacing methods. And it sure as hell succeeded. But how did it know? Was it with me at my friend's place that night, observing what went on? Could it read my thoughts? Or sense the anxiety I carried around pennies? This was the only penny I kept around on my dresser until it's unex-plained disappearance. It was an acknowledgment of the malevolent trickster, in a way that says, "I'm keeping eyes on you too."

Oddly enough and luckily for me, pennies were phased out of Canadian currency in 2013. Thankfully they are now a distant figment of the past, yet this horrifying experience and memory seared into every fiber of my being is what continues to haunt me for the rest of my life.

Submitted by Vanessa of Arcanum.Iter

JAMES DEAN DEATH CAR

Do you believe a car can be cursed? After hearing the infamous story of James Dean's death car, you just might.

James Dean (1931–1955) was an American actor best known for his roles in *East of Eden* and *Rebel Without a Cause*. However, his young life was cut short when he died in a tragic car accident. Prior to his death, he began an interest in motorsports, even competing in car racing events. He had to take a break from racing due to filming a movie (*Giant*); however, he missed racing, so he entered himself into an upcoming event in California and purchased a new Porsche 550 Spyder in preparation. Not long after purchasing the car, he showed it to fellow actor Alec Guinness. Ominously, Guinness told Dean that he should not get in the car at all; otherwise he will be dead by next week. Dean laughed off the warning, but perhaps he should have taken this warning a little more seriously.

A week later, while en route to the racing event, Dean met his end. Driving on Route 446 (now SR 46), a truck driven by Donald Turnupseed turned onto the road, and Dean wasn't able to stop in time. Tires squealing, the Porsche slammed into the side of the truck. Dean was trapped in the car, deceased from several different fatal wounds. Turnupseed suffered minor injuries. Despite the crash and the car being severely damaged, the engine of the car was intact. George Barris, a Hollywood movie car customizer, purchased the car after insurance claimed it a total loss. While transporting the car to his shop, it fell off the trailer and broke the leg (or the hip depending on sources) of one of the mechanics.

Barris sold some parts to Troy McHenry and Williams Eschrid, who used those parts in their own racing cars, which they drove to participate in the Pomona Race in 1956. Eschrid's vehicle lost control mid-race and crashed. He survived the crash, but the car itself was completely totaled. McHenry also lost control and drove into the only tree on the racetrack. Unfortunately, McHenry lost his life that day. This solidified the rumors of James Dean's Porsche being cursed.

Barris had also sold two wheels from Dean's car to another individual, which, if rumors are true, blew at the same time, causing another accident. It was supposedly at this point that Barris decided to just lock the car away. However, the California Highway Patrol asked Barris if they could display the wrecked body of the vehicle at their safety exhibits. This proved not to be a very good idea, as the garage that housed the car prior to one of the exhibits caught fire. Oddly, however, the car itself sustained no fire damage. During another exhibit, the vehicle fell off its display, injuring bystanders. And finally, while transporting the vehicle on a flatbed truck, the driver had an accident and was crushed by the Porsche.

Death and accidents seemed to surround the car no matter where it went. In 1960 the car was on display in Miami. Mysteriously, the truck hauling the wrecked vehicle disappeared while en route back to California.

While the whereabouts of the car remain unknown to this day, occasionally posts pop up on sites such as eBay, claiming to be parts of the infamous car. Good luck to anyone who may come into possession of any piece of this cursed death car.

THE MOVING BIG BIRD STATUE

The following story was told to me by my husband and took place when he was a child:

One day my dad brought home what we called the "big bird statue." I don't remember if it actually was the Big Bird character from Sesame Street, *but I assume it was, as it was a big statue of a bird with its arms out to the sides. The statue was made out of something like ceramic and was about three to four feet tall and painted yellow. We had a stone chimney grill on the side of the house, and my dad put the statue on top of that.*

Every day that we would walk outside, the arms of the statue would be in a different position, I shit you not. My sisters can vouch for this. My mom didn't believe us and tried to say maybe a squirrel was jumping on the statue or something, causing it to look like it moved. But come on, it was a freaking statue, it shouldn't have been able to move its arms like that. We even tried ourselves to see if we could move the arms, but it was a statue and couldn't be bent or moved.

One day my sisters, several of our friends and myself were walking up and down the street. Every time we would pass by our driveway and look down at the statue, it would be in a different position. We know it really happened because we were all seeing the same thing.

One night during a winter storm, the wind blew the statue over, and it broke. We have no idea what the history of the statue was. We assume my dad brought it home from the city dump, where he was working at the time. He would sometimes bring home things that were still in their packages or weren't broken or damaged. But no clue about the statue.

What makes this story so interesting to me is the fact that it wasn't just one person experiencing the paranormal activity. It was multiple people over an extended period of time. This is such a simple story, and the activity wasn't anything that caused harm to anyone; however, something about this story and the statue has always felt very sinister to me. Part of me is glad that the statue broke and it didn't have the opportunity to cause any serious chaos in my husband's childhood, but the investigator in me wishes it were still around so I could see what it was all about.

13TH FLOOR HAUNTED OBJECTS

Husband and wife Dennis and Maggie Hagan are paranormal investigators based out of Ohio. They also have their own production company, 13th Floor Haunted Media Productions. Oh, and they have a huge collection of haunted objects that they keep locked away in their basement.

They began collecting haunted objects around 2019, and their collection continues to grow. They frequently host live streams on social media as they investigate their collection. In fact, one of the scariest moments they've had with one of their haunted items happened while they were on Facebook live. They were investigating a jar of dirt from the property of famed serial killer Ed Gein. A viewer asked who Ed Gein and his mother were. As Dennis was explaining to the viewer, he suddenly felt an intense burning on his left shoulder. He asked Maggie to look at it, and when she lowered his shirt over his shoulder, she saw a scratch across it. When she touched it, the scratch began to burn even more. Another standout moment regarding Ed's dirt is when Dennis asked the spirit of Ed to say his name. Dennis states that, clear as day, "Ed" came through the spirit box. As if that's not creepy enough, one time Dennis and Maggie had a friend over investigating their objects. When they pulled out the jar of dirt to investigate and called forth Ed Gein, their friend said she felt like two hands were choking her neck.

While Ed Gein's property dirt is certainly a standout object in their collection, a possibly demonic doll named Hellen is even more so. They acquired Hellen from a paranormal investigator friend of theirs who also collects haunted objects. This friend got the doll from a man in California. Unfortunately, there isn't much history surrounding the doll; however, Dennis says there is a high-ranking demon possessing the doll. He said he's had some experiences that make him think this, as well as different mediums who have told him of something dark and sinister being attached to the doll. Her energy is so strong that people watching their live videos will feel sick and nauseated simply from seeing her on video. Hellen seems to have the ability to cause people to feel very aggressive. Dennis says that one time after spending time investigating the doll, he got an intrusive image of himself ramming Maggie's head into the wall. Another time he got the strong urge to slam the case that encloses Hellen into the ground, almost as if to free her from her protective barrier. Another time, Maggie was in the haunted object room alone, taking inventory of the items. She began to lose track of time and felt very spacy as her eyes began to burn, forcing her to leave the room.

Another item Maggie and Dennis have in their collection is what they refer to as Betty's Boots. They received these boots from the same friend who had Hellen. The story they were told is that the boots belonged to a fifty-five-year-old woman who was involved with the occult. Betty was supposedly a wealthy, proper woman who had a hobby of trying to contact the dead. Whenever they've tried to contact Betty, an intelligent woman comes through their spirit box, answering their questions.

And finally, another object in their collection is a highchair from the 1900s. As if the highchair being haunted wasn't weird enough, this highchair is made from a spirit board. When you flip up the wooden tray table, you will see that it's actually an old spirit board, or Ouija board, that has been cut and fitted to the highchair. The story that Maggie and Dennis were told is that two children, ages one and three, were associated with this highchair and died. The story states that the children were tormented by a demon possessing the chair before they passed away. I don't know about you, but I certainly hope that isn't the case. While telling this story over a live video, they heard a voice on their spirit box say "they are dead." When asked what the entity would do if Dennis threw holy water on the chair, a loud hiss came through the spirit box. They've also received growling and "devil" come through.

I reached out to Dennis and Maggie after doing some research on haunted objects in my state of Ohio. I found a news article and learned they are also in Ohio, about two hours away from me. We had a video call to meet each other and decided that I would come to their home the following week to investigate their items for myself. Unfortunately, a couple of days later, sickness hit their home, and we had to cancel my visit. I'm not saying that it's paranormal, but it is interesting timing. We decided instead that we would do another video call and I would investigate remotely with them. The day came for our virtual investigation, and we had a hard time connecting our video call. Again, I'm not saying this is paranormal, but the timing sure is weird.

Once we got settled on the call, I asked about investigating with Hellen. Dennis mentioned that he would need to get her out of her case and in that moment stated that he felt very cold on his left shoulder. I remembered that he was just getting over being sick, and his energetic boundaries probably weren't at their highest, so maybe it was a better idea to not remove a potentially demonic doll from her protective case.

We decided instead to begin with the jar of Ed Gein's property dirt. Dennis and Maggie told me that not only have they had the spirit of Ed come through, but that his mother, Augusta, and even some of his victims have come through the spirit box or interacted with their other equipment. After placing a para-light next to the jar, they turned on the spirit box, and we began asking questions. A para-light is a type of EMF meter that lights up different colors depending on the strength of the electromagnetic frequency.

Maggie: Ed, would you like to talk?

Dennis: We have a couple devices you can talk on, Ed. Or light the device up (points to the para-light). I know you're here. You've said your name before.

Spirit box: Mom. (Para-light illuminates brightly.)

Cherise: Is this Ed's mom who we're speaking with? (The para-light goes nuts.)

Cherise: Can you please step away from the light for a moment so we know it's you? (Para-light immediately stops glowing.)

Dennis: Augusta, you here? If you're here, can you say your name on this device?

Spirit box: You ready?

All of us: Yes, we're ready. (Silence from the spirit box, and the light doesn't light up again.)

Cherise: Augusta, you can use the light for yes and no responses if that's easier. Does that sound good? (No response.)

At this point things go pretty quiet, so Dennis picks up the phone and begins to walk around the room, showing me various items from their collection. Suddenly, Dennis and Maggie both exclaim, "What was that?" They asked me if I was just humming, to which I reply no. I was totally silent on my end. They said they heard a female humming.

Dennis: Who was just humming? Can you tell us? (Dennis and Maggie both feel a surge of energy in the room.)

Dennis: Please give us a sign you're here. (At this point Maggie and Dennis hear a little kid come through the phone; however, I didn't hear anything. As they're telling me about the voice, they tell me they heard it a second time.)

Spirit box: It worked! (Para-light lights up again.)

Dennis: Are you setting off the light?

Spirit box: Yes.

Dennis: What are you trying to say?

Spirit box: Maybe.

Dennis: Who is the little kid that was laughing? Can you let us know you're here? Light up that light again.

Spirit box: For sure.

Dennis: Okay, can you come through and talk? Tell me your name. (Para-light lights up.)

Dennis: Who's setting the light off? Can you tell me your name? Is it one of the little boys attached to one of these objects? (No response.)

At this point Dennis says he wants to poke at Hellen a bit. He asks her to spell her name on the Onvoy (a device that acts almost like a digital Ouija board) or say his name through the spirit box. A female voice comes through the spirit box, but it's unclear what it says. There is no response after that. The connection on our video call starts to worsen. I don't personally provoke spirits, but Dennis seems to be in a bit of a provoking mood, so he turns his aim back to the jar of dirt and Ed Gein.

Dennis: Ed, I know you're here and attached to that dirt. How did it feel to be locked up in an insane asylum? Did you like it? Did you like murdering those victims? Did it feel good? (Dennis says he hears "yes, it did" come through the spirit box, but I didn't hear it.)

After a bit more provoking of Ed, it doesn't seem any activity is occurring, so I suggest we investigate Betty's Boots. As Dennis reaches for the boots, the video quality becomes absolutely abysmal.

Dennis: Betty, can you come talk to us? Light up that device next to your boots? (A female voice comes through unintelligibly on the spirit box.)

At this point the connection on our call becomes so bad that I have to reluctantly end our session. There seems to be some activity surrounding the items in Dennis and Maggie's collection. I am planning on meeting up with them in the future to investigate some of these items in person. I will say, having investigated haunted objects within a collection a handful of times, I do think there may be a bit of a hindrance. With so much potential activity, spirits and entities, it seems like the energy can be a bit chaotic or scattered. I saw this as well when investigating at the Archive of the Afterlife. It's almost as if the energy and entities are competing with one another for who gets to communicate in that moment. I believe there is a benefit to investigating one haunted item at a time, in a room by itself, separated from the rest of the collection. Not only will the energy be less erratic, but when responses or activity occur, you can be more certain that it is in fact coming from that specific item or spirit rather than coming from one of the many other items in the vicinity.

THE BONE

As someone who likes to bring home random bones I find in the woods, the following story really creeped me out.

Point Lookout to West Virginia

1987

While on day patrol and checking fishing licenses at the Point, I was called over to a family. They're on the beach just north beyond the rock revetment on the Potomac side. The man told me that they had found a large bone sticking out of the sand while they were setting up their poles.

He retrieved it from his tackle box. It was a partially dark bone with some white areas on one end. It was about six inches in length and about an inch and half to two inches in diameter. It was obviously broken at either end.

He handed it to me, and I recognized it to be a bone by the cellular structures at either end. At first, I thought it may be a large animal. Possibly a deer, cow, or a pig. Those animals were prevalent in the area for years. The gentleman didn't want it back. So I took it and placed it into a paper lunch bag I had in my truck. I didn't think much of it at the time. I didn't report it. But I did tell and show it to others later at the shop during shift change. They dismissed it as well, thinking it was an animal bone. I held on to it for some reason, and it sat in my personal truck until I went back to school in late August.

My apartment at West Virginia University was on High Street in a building not far from the downtown campus. Unfortunately, it was on the fourth floor. So I was in pretty good shape with all the stairs. No elevator!

The bone eventually ended up in my apartment along with one of my EVP tapes from the park. I had previously arranged to loan the tape to the Speech Therapist Department at the University to analyze. To see if the unexplained voices on the tape were of human origin. After a few weeks they got back to me. They determined that the voices were within the range and frequency of the human voice. The tape was one of my original lighthouse recordings. Unfortunately, I no longer have that particular recording. It was destroyed by my first wife after she discovered what it was. She claimed it had very bad energy around it and didn't want it around our son.

On a cold fall night in November, I had a long night of studying and getting ready for exams. I crawled in the bed, which was a simple mattress on the floor of my room. I left the window open in the room since my roommate continuously liked the heat blazing hot in her end of the apartment. She was Greek. My room was at the end of a long hallway directly across from the apartment entrance. The apartment door had a large hole cut in it for a peephole. But it was never installed. So the light of the hallway on the fourth floor shined through. I covered it over with masking tape, but the light still shone through but not as bright. This would be important as my story continues.

I was very tired and fell asleep quickly. However, I was awakened by noises coming from the hallway. Was it Chrissy coming home late again. Maybe drunk, I thought, stumbling through. Then the noises, banging, and rustling sounded like it was at my door and in the room with me now. Was she drunk? I just lay there with my back towards the noise, facing the far wall. I was getting ready to yell at her, but the noise stopped. Then nothing for several minutes. Just before falling asleep again, I felt a heaviness, a pressure come over me. Then the sound of breathing was very close. Was this Chrissy? But it gave me a disturbing feeling. Every ounce of me became aware. Still facing towards the wall, I calculated my response. I knew that the cord to the light on my bed table was an arm's reach away. All I had to do was to turn, reach up with my hand, and pull on the cord.

Then the air in the room became very oppressive. Very similar to what I have felt before at the park. I felt a presence, and it was not friendly. I then became aware of the feeling of dread. I finally decided to turn around to switch on the light. When I did, I opened my eyes, looked into the room, towards the room door, and saw nothing but black! When the light switched on, it lit up my bedroom and part of the hallway in the apartment. My room door was open.

I swear I had closed my room door. I usually did. But when the lights came on, the door was wide open. What was strange was when I turned around before the light came on, I saw no light anywhere. The room was pitch black. Now, I could see the apartment door and the tape-covered hole. The door was outlined by light in the building's hallway, and the light was glowing through the hole in the door. I thought to myself as I lay there, what the hell was blocking the light? I felt a bad feeling and heaviness.

I got up and walked down the apartment hallway to the kitchen, looked around, then to the bathroom, and the living room. I passed Chrissy's door. I could hear her snoring. All seemed secure and fine in the rest of the apartment.

Returning to my room, I found the bone lying on the floor next to my dresser. Previously it was on top of the dresser, pushed back against the stack of books there. It was then I thought that there was maybe a connection with what just happened. I did not sleep the rest of the night.

The next day after classes, I stopped by the archaeology lab. I had taken classes prior, and I knew the grad students there. I showed them the bone. They examined it and with 90% assurance said that it was an upper part of a human femur. They said it appeared to be very old by the coloring and the texture. I told them where it had come from. The one grad student told me that I should return it to where I had found it and bury it. I laughed and said that I would be doing just that this Christmas break. He was serious. Stating that he believed that traces of whomever it belonged to was still with it. I told him a quick history of the Point. The three of us continued to talk for a while. I thanked them for their expertise and left. A few days later, I bumped into them at the Bullpen, an establishment on Sunnyside, and bought them a few beers. I did not tell them what had happened in the apartment. Didn't want to go there at the time.

I returned home for break in mid-December and to the Point for a week or two of work. I told Jim and Mark about the bone and what had happened that night in my apartment. Jim took it seriously, but

Mark just laughed it off as BS. He was always skeptical, and that's fine.

Near the entrance of the park is a memorial to the approximately four thousand Confederate soldiers who perished at the Point during its eighteen months of operation as a prisoner-of-war camp. I decided to bury it there within those gates. Even though I wasn't sure where it may have come from or whom it belonged to, it was consecrated ground. An official cemetery within a reasonable distance of the place it was found. The original burial plots of the prisoners were exhumed in the years following the war. The remains recovered were moved to the memorial location. Rest in peace.

– Submitted by John Hopf, from a segment of his upcoming book with Beyond the Fray Publishing

THE TV WAVED BACK

This next story had been emailed to me and brings up the theory of sleepiness and paranormal activity. Was this simply an instance of a drowsy mind causing this person to see something strange? Or, as some theorize, did the sleepy mind lower their guarded conscious mind just enough for them to be able to perceive the Other?

One night I was relaxing on my rocker before bed, lights off, mellow music playing with a couple of candles burning. I noticed that I could vaguely make out my reflection in the television screen, a television that was given to me two weeks prior because mine suddenly died. Being a bit silly, I began to swing my arms around and wave at my reflection. After a few minutes, I noticed I was getting drowsy and stood up to go to bed when I realized my reflection was STILL seated and was STILL waving at me. I turned on the light and inspected the reflection, which was perfectly normal. I tossed a towel over the screen for the night. I never had a reoccurrence of the event from that night until I acquired a new television...a few days later.

THE INSIDIOUS SCRYING PENDANT

The following story is a perfect example of the importance of being aware of the energies and entities that you're reaching out to, and knowing when to close down a session, set boundaries and cleanse your space. It's also important to know your limits, as the person in this story did. Whenever you bring fear and hesitation into your investigation or spirit practice, you increase your chances of attracting something sinister or trickster-like.

Full disclosure and please don't think less of me, I was young and fool-ish. There was a point in my life, when I was very young (still in my teens) where I was opened up a bit too much psychically and had drawn too much attention to myself and was plagued by a lot of paranormal activity and different entities. Things would move around in my house, knocks, bangs, very trippy energy in the apartment, like the walls and floors kept moving, only remedied by constant burning of incense. The old apartment had been part of an old burnt theatre and was across the street from a very old cemetery. Most paranormal phenomena didn't bother me, I was used to it, but it was a lot. My friends were quite scared of the apartment.

Some entities/energies/spirits I encountered were good, some neutral, some fun trickster types, and some were a bit more...insidious. It got to a point where I had a hard time trusting my own intuition or felt my senses were a little clouded as though I couldn't tell if an entity was malicious or not, but I suspected something more...negative around. I decided to try to get a glimpse of what I thought was perhaps a negative entity (trying to present itself as something else) by using a black obsidian scrying mirror pendant. It was large for a necklace, but still fit in the palm of my hand.

In the mirror while scrying, I saw the features of what I can only describe as inhuman, but not in the friendly neighbourhood nature spirit way...I have had many encounters with nonhuman "elementals," friendly and frightfully territorial; this was not one of them. I don't want to describe in detail what I saw, but it did frighten me (and I was USED to seeing things). Ever since, I could not look into that scrying mirror. It felt tainted by that thing that I saw, like its gaze was etched in the stone. Like it could see me through the mirror. I trust in obsidian for protection, and even this seemed too gross. No matter what I did, no amount of cleansing worked, and in the end I had to bury it in the earth, and left it forgotten somewhere.

I got my shields up, cleansed and purified the space. Made sure the barriers were up to throw out anything that had a low vibration that meant harm. I admit that I shut off a lot after that. It took me many, many years to be able to trust my intuition again. I have been too afraid to scry in mirrors ever since. I will only use water now because I can drain it when it's done, and I set the parameters for what I am seeking or whom I want to speak to.

– Submitted by Anonymous

Chapter Seven

WITCH BOTTLES FOR PROTECTION

WITCH BOTTLES themselves aren't inherently haunted, although I'm sure there are probably at least one or two haunted witch bottles floating around somewhere in the world. While these bottles aren't necessarily a haunted object, they are an object, and they can help protect you against unwanted spirits or entities, so I wanted to include them in this book.

WHAT ARE WITCH BOTTLES?

Traditionally, a witch bottle is something that was made to help ward off evil witches and magick. However, it can be used to ward off malicious spirits and entities as well. The bottle would either be buried on the property or would be hidden somewhere within the home, such as under a floorboard or in the rafters. You can place your bottle wherever you feel is intuitively best.

The practice of witch bottles seems to have originated in Europe, particularly during the seventeenth century, and was brought over to

North America. There are lots of different ways to make a witch bottle, and if you search books or the internet, you will come across lots of different ways or ingredients. But they essentially all do the same thing.

Some witch bottles call for the use of some bodily fluid or item included within it. The idea is that the spirits and energy will be attracted to the bottle, sensing you within it, rather than coming right for you. Some people choose to include blood, urine, spit, hair or fingernails. But this isn't necessarily required for the bottle to be effective. An effective alternative would be to include a small piece of paper with your name or your family name, or simply breathe into the bottle before you close it up.

The bottle is considered active as long as it remains hidden and/or unbroken.

HOW TO MAKE A WITCH BOTTLE

What you need:

- A glass bottle of some sort, with a lid
- Nails and/or screws (to act as a defense against the energy or spirit, to send it away or trap it within the bottle)
- Water from a natural source (to act as an energy amplifier and cleansing)
- Vinegar (to cleanse and snuff out the energy)
- Something shiny like glitter or tiny mirrored beads (the shiny reflective object attracts the spirit and energy to the bottle)
- Salt (is both protective and cleansing)

What you do:

- Fill the bottle about halfway with the nails or screws, glitter or other shiny objects, several pinches of salt, and if you choose to include it, some of your personal item (hair, spit, etc., or the piece of name paper).
- Fill the rest of the bottle up with equal parts vinegar and water.
- At this point, if you choose, you would place your breath into the bottle before closing the lid.
- Hold the bottle in your hand and spend some time taking slow deep breaths.
- Envision the bottle trapping and repelling any unwanted spirits or energy.
- Trust and know that you are safe.
- Place or hide the bottle in the location of your choosing.

Chapter Eight

HAUNTED OBJECT TAROT SPREADS

TAROT CARDS AREN'T JUST for the living, you can utilize them for so many types of readings and to garner so much information or insight. Not only can you read tarot cards for ghosts but you can read them to learn a little more about the haunted objects you come across, and their entities. If you want to delve deeper into reading tarot for ghosts, including tarot card meanings for ghost hunting, check out my book *The Witch's Guide to Ghost Hunting*.

GETTING TO KNOW THE OBJECT'S HISTORY

Use this spread if you already know, or you suspect, that the item is haunted.

1. Who first owned this item?
2. Who last owned this item?
3. Why did they get rid of this item?
4. What main energy or emotion is connected to this item?
5. How does this item affect the living?

6. How should I best deal with this item?
7. What is something big that happened in this item's history that might be contributing to its current energy or haunting?
8. How does the energy, entity or spirit of this item manifest itself?

GETTING TO KNOW THE OBJECTS HISTORY TAROT SPREAD

1 2 3 4 7 8 5 6

GETTING TO KNOW THE SPIRIT ATTACHED

Use this spread once you've established there is in fact a spirit or entity attached to the object.

1. Why are you attached to this object?
2. How do you feel about being attached to this object?
3. What do you need from me?
4. How can I help you?
5. How to best communicate with you?
6. What is your personality like (pull one to three cards)?
7. What do you like?
8. What do you dislike?

GETTING TO KNOW THE SPIRIT ATTACHED TAROT SPREAD

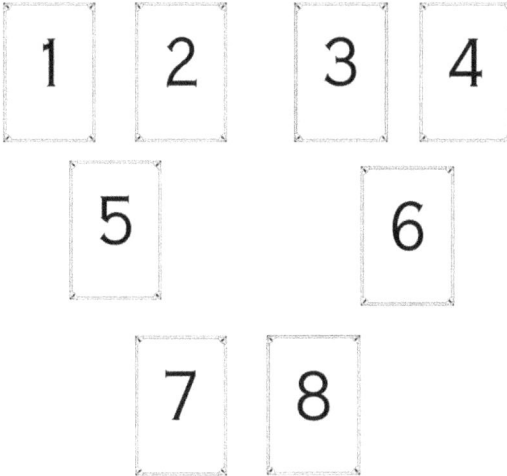

```
┌───┐ ┌───┐   ┌───┐ ┌───┐
│ 1 │ │ 2 │   │ 3 │ │ 4 │
└───┘ └───┘   └───┘ └───┘

   ┌───┐         ┌───┐
   │ 5 │         │ 6 │
   └───┘         └───┘

      ┌───┐ ┌───┐
      │ 7 │ │ 8 │
      └───┘ └───┘
```

Chapter Nine

PENDULUM FOR HAUNTED OBJECTS

A PENDULUM IS a multiuse spiritual tool that can be utilized for work in the paranormal. There are many styles of pendulums ranging from very fancy and expensive to extremely simple. Ultimately, a pendulum is any weighted object on the end of a string or a chain so as to be able to swing freely. I do think it's important to feel connected with your spiritual tools, so finding a pendulum you like might be a good idea. However, tying something like a ring to the end of a shoestring could work in a pinch.

There are theories as to how a pendulum actually works, but the one that makes the most sense to me is that our ideomotor response is reacting to what our intuition is communicating. An ideomotor response is when part of your body responds or reacts to something being conveyed by your subconscious. It's utilized frequently in hypnotherapy as a way for the hypnotherapist to communicate directly with the client's subconscious. For example, the person under hypnosis will be told that when asked yes or no questions, they will lift the left pointer finger slightly for no and their right pointer finger for yes. This way, the person under hypnosis can stay in a trance while still being able to communicate. The movements made with the ideomotor response are done unconsciously. Basically, these movements are slight micro-movements that your conscious mind isn't even aware is occurring. I believe this is how we get communication through tools like pendulums, dowsing rods or even the planchette on spirit boards. Our intuition is conveying something to our body, and in response our body reacts with small micro-movements that move the pendulum, rods or planchette.

To work with a pendulum, you first need to decipher which movements correlate to which responses. Hold your pendulum in between your fingers so it is hanging freely. Some prefer to hold the pendulum with their dominant hand, others with their nondominant hand. Do what feels intuitively best for you. Take a deep breath or two and allow yourself to feel centered. Out loud, or in your head, ask the pendulum to show you the movement for a yes response. Wait a moment, and you should soon begin to feel the pendulum sway. Make note of the movement and then bring the pendulum to a stop. Repeat this to figure out the movements for yes, no, and maybe, and reword your question.

Pendulum use can take some work to feel comfortable with, and it takes practice, so be patient with yourself. Some people want to know how they can be sure it's actually their intuition communicating with them verses them consciously moving the pendulum. Try asking your pendulum a question and actively force the incorrect response. For example, I would ask the pendulum, "Is my name Sally?" and then purposely move the pendulum in the direction of yes. Then I would ask again, "Is my name Sally?" and let the pendulum move of its own accord. The forced movement of the pendulum should feel different than when allowing the pendulum to do its thing. It might only be a slight difference, but with practice you should be able to begin to notice when you might be forcing the movement rather than letting it organically happen.

SCOUTING FOR HAUNTED OBJECTS

After reading this book and the stories within, perhaps you've decided you want to try to find your very own haunted object to bring home. Your pendulum can help with this! Next time you go to a secondhand store or garage sale, bring your pendulum with you. You can either have the pendulum lead you to a potentially haunted item or figure out if an item you feel drawn to is haunted.

To have the pendulum lead you to a haunted object, start at the front of the store or garage sale. Hold out your pendulum and ask it if there are any haunted objects at that location. If the pendulum swings to yes, you can then ask it to swing in the direction you should walk to find the object. This method can take some time, as you will periodically need to stop and double-check which direction to go. It's almost like a game of Hot and Cold or Marco Polo. Once you get to the spot you believe the haunted object to be, you can start naming objects in the vicinity and see which one the pendulum indicates yes for. Remember, while haunted objects aren't uncommon, not every store or garage sale is going to have one every time. Occasionally your pendulum will indicate that there are no haunted items at that particular place.

If walking around a public space with a pendulum swinging around isn't your style and you want to be a little more discreet, you can utilize your intuition first, followed by the pendulum to double-check. For example, browse the store or sale as you normally would, and if you happen to come across an item that sends your paranormal senses buzzing, pull out the pendulum and ask if the object is indeed haunted.

This process can work as well for objects you might be considering purchasing online. With the image of the object you're considering buying pulled up on your screen, take out your pendulum and ask if the item is legitimately haunted. Utilizing a pendulum in this manner can hopefully help you weed out objects that might actually be haunted verses an object from someone trying to make a quick buck but that isn't actually haunted.

COMMUNICATING WITH A HAUNTED OBJECT AND SPIRIT

Let's say you've brought home your very own haunted item, or maybe you're at a location that has a haunted item. Either way, you want to communicate with the spirit or energy attached. A pendulum can help you with this. You can ask the spirit or object yes and no questions to facilitate communication, or you can print out or purchase a pendulum board. A pendulum board is somewhat similar to a spirit or Ouija board; however, the letters and numbers are usually arranged differently, and you use your pendulum instead of a planchette. This method can take a little longer as the pendulum swings from letter to letter spelling a word, but with this method you can get information like names or dates or other information you might not be able to get with simple yes or no questions.

I always like to have a couple of different tools out when communicating with spirits, so you might find it helpful when doing pendulum sessions to also set out something like an EMF meter or run a spirit box. Sometimes I will confirm pendulum responses by pulling a few tarot cards as well. Have fun with it, mixing and matching ghost-hunting tools with spiritual tools like the pendulum.

Chapter Ten

HOW TO CLEANSE HAUNTED OBJECTS

SOMETIMES YOU MIGHT COME across an item or bring one home that has energy attached to it, but you don't really want to have a haunted object. You like the object but would prefer it had no attachment. Or maybe having a haunted object was fun for a little while, but now the energy attached has gotten too intense. Luckily, there are some things you can do to cleanse the energy. I want to note that it's important to really think about *why* you want to cleanse this object. Remember, more than likely this object and its spirit didn't ask for you to bring it home, and the spirit was attached prior to you acquiring it. So it's kind of rude to just evict the spirit simply because you don't want it attached anymore. I feel the only time to really cleanse an object of its former energy is if it's causing you or your family distress, or if there isn't a conscious entity attached. Some objects simply hold residual energy, and similar to dusting the physical dust off an object, just need a good cleanse. Other items house a conscious or sentient being who may be quite fond of the item and not wish to leave it. In those instances, weigh your options. Sometimes the best thing to do might be to pass the object on to someone more experienced rather than kicking the entity out of the object.

Once you've decided that you do in fact wish to remove energy from the object, there are several pretty easy ways to do so. Of course, a more powerful entity with strong ties to the object will require a little more. In these instances, either refer to my book *The Witch's Guide to Ghost Hunting* or reach out to someone with experiences in these areas to help you.

Not only can you utilize the following tools and techniques to cleanse an object, but most of them can be tweaked to cleanse your own energy or the energy of your home. No matter the method you choose to cleanse and clear, you might choose to say a prayer or some words while doing it. Your words don't have to be fancy, something as simple as "I now cleanse and remove any negative or unwanted energy from this object. Any energy that is not of my highest good is no longer permitted to be attached to this object" will suffice.

SELENITE WAND

I usually don't go anywhere without a selenite wand on me. Technically, most of the selenite wands you see available are made from satin spar but labeled as selenite. I don't see a problem with this, as both selenite and satin spar are from the gypsum family and have basically the same energetic properties. Selenite wands are excellent at cleansing and clearing. When I'm working with a selenite wand to cleanse energy, I almost think of it like an eraser or sponge scrubbing away any energy that is no longer needed or that is heavy and dark. Take the wand, and holding it a few inches away from the object, scrub the energy field with it. As you're scrubbing, feel or envision the energy surrounding the object becoming squeaky clean.

I find that cleansing with a selenite wand works particularly well for objects I get secondhand that sometimes feel heavy with residual energy or the energy of all the people before me who handled the object.

PENDULUM

Pendulums really are such a great multiuse tool. Not only can you divine with them, but you can utilize them for cleansing as well. Not only can you use pendulums to cleanse haunted objects, but you can use them to clear the energy of your aura or room as well. I even use them to clear the energy from my tarot decks when they're feeling mucky.

Hold your pendulum in your fingers as if you're going to do a spirit session with it, and hold the pendulum a few inches above the object. Actively move the pendulum in a counterclockwise direction until it's spinning at a decent speed. Then allow the pendulum to slow down on its own until it comes to a complete stop. Once it stops, the energy has been cleared. If you're clearing the energy of a large object, like a piece of furniture, you might need to place the pendulum over a few different spots on the object and repeat these steps until all energy has been cleared.

Technically, any pendulum can work for this; however, I find that a pendulum made with something like clear quartz tends to work best.

SMOKE

Smoke cleansing has been used by people all over the world for hundreds and hundreds of years, and it's quite effective. You can either burn incense from a stick, loose resin on a charcoal disc, or dried herbs in a stick or bundle. You might find it easiest to keep your smoke source on a table while you hold the haunted object above it and move it through the smoke. Of course, this only works for smaller objects. For larger objects that you can't hold above the smoke, you can simply hold the smoke source in your hand and waft it around the object.

A lot of resources will tell you to use white sage to cleanse and clear entities; however, the use of white sage is a closed practice reserved for specific Indigenous American groups. So unless you are part of that group, it's best to use another herb, and there are plenty to choose from. Rosemary, mugwort and thyme are some of my favorites to burn.

SALT

Salt is another of those tools that is very multifunctional. Salt not only protects, but cleanses as well. Have a small item like a piece of jewelry? Set it in a bowl of salt for twenty-four hours. For larger items like furniture, you could sprinkle some salt into the drawers. For medium-sized objects like dolls, you can create a circle of salt and set the item inside it for twenty-four hours. For me personally, I don't find that salt alone completely cleanses and clears a spirit or residual energy from an object. I usually combine salt with one of the other methods included here.

SIGILS

Sigils are magickal symbols that can be utilized for many different purposes, including clearing and cleansing. You can draw a clearing sigil onto a piece of paper and set your haunted object on top of it for twenty-four hours, or you can draw the sigil directly onto the object itself. You can draw the sigil with an actual pen or marker, for example, or if you don't want to leave a mark on the item, you can draw the sigil with your finger. In my book *The Witch's Guide to Ghost Hunting*, I have an entire section on sigils, including how to make your own. But you can also find resources online for how to make them.

Chapter Eleven

YOU HAVE A HAUNTED OBJECT, NOW WHAT?

You've acquired your very own haunted object. Now what do you do with it?

BOUNDARIES

First and foremost, it's important to set some boundaries with the spirit. Boundaries are great whether you're investigating a location or welcoming your new haunted object into your home. Heck, boundaries are great to set with the living people in your life as well.

You have to decide what you are and are not willing to put up with. Do you mind if the spirit wanders your home? What about if they make sounds like footsteps or voices? Is physical touch okay or something you want to steer clear of? Sit down with your new haunted object and literally have a conversation with it. Tell the object and spirit what is allowed and what isn't, and remember, boundaries can always be lessened or increased at any point you feel the need.

You may choose to set some physical boundaries as well, such as keeping the object in a circle of salt or placing it in a blessed container like a glass case. Some people prefer this option, as they feel they get to interact with the entity on their own terms rather than letting the spirit potentially have free rein of the home or space. For more rowdy spirits, this might be the better option rather than verbal boundaries alone.

If the spirit seems to push the boundaries, remember you are the one in control. You can either set firmer boundaries, or at that point decide if it might be time to get rid of the object. If you do get rid of the object, I feel it's only right to let others know of your experiences with the item. Not everyone wants to bring a haunted object into their home or life.

COMMUNICATION

Part of the experience of having a haunted item is the communication. Take some time a couple of times a week to interact with the spirit. You can communicate and interact with the haunted object the same way you would if you were trying to connect with the spirits at a haunted location. Take out some ghost-hunting equipment like an EMF meter and spirit box and start talking to the entity attached to the object. I love to pair metaphysical methods with my traditional ghost-hunting equipment, so while I have a spirit box running and EMF meter turned on, I will pull some tarot cards. Have fun with it! Keep a journal of the interactions and responses you receive from the spirit. And remember, some spirits take some warming up to. Just like some living people take a little longer to open up and really get comfortable with someone, the same can be said for spirits.

While boundaries are important, so is respect. Don't treat the entity attached to the object like some weird party trick. Treat them like you would a guest in your home. As always though, if you feel like your energy is being encroached upon or the spirit is doing things that make you feel uncomfortable or unsafe, set boundaries, cleanse, or get rid of the object. While you want to be respectful towards the spirit, you also want to keep your guard up a little bit. You both are getting to know each other. Don't let your guard down too much, as the spirit may not always be as friendly as it first appears.

OFFERINGS

It's a good idea when communicating with spirits of any kind, no matter if it's a spirit connected to an object, a spirit at a location, or even a spirit you work with in your magickal practice, to leave them an offering. This is a sign of respect and kind of the equivalent of showing up to someone's house for the first time and bringing a gift. Some spirits enjoyed certain things in life and appreciate the gesture of you offering that up to them even though they're now in spirit form. By you giving them this gift, they may be more apt to speak with you or make their presence known. There is also the belief that spirits can utilize the energy from the offering in order to communicate or interact with you. Some spirits that are a little more playful, assertive or even trickster-like want offerings, or they will act out until they get them.

Try to learn the history of the spirit attached to the item, or ask them when you're communicating with them what type of offering they might like. If it's within your means, it's always a good idea to leave the spirit something they actually like. However, there are lots of offerings you can choose from that plenty of spirits enjoy, such as tobacco, coffee, wine, flowers, coins, candy and water. Some spirits enjoy nonphysical items as well, such as music or singing, writing a poem, acts of service (cleaning, volunteering). The more you interact with your haunted object, the more you'll get to know the spirit's likes and dislikes.

Chapter Twelve

EXTRAS

CURRENT HAUNTED ITEMS FOR SALE

To GIVE you an idea of the types of haunted objects that are for sale online at the time of this writing, I thought it would be fun to include descriptions of some of the more interesting listings. Keep in mind, a ton of these are probably fabricated in order to make a sale; however, some of them could be quite real.

Let's talk about dybbuk boxes really quick. I wasn't sure where to put it in the book, but I will address it here in case you happen to come across any of these items for sale on your own search for a haunted or cursed object. Dybbuk boxes were popularized by television and social media after a 2003 eBay listing went viral. Kevin Mannis claimed to have a dybbuk box and that it was possessed by a demon called a dybbuk. The only problem is, Kevin completely fabricated the story, and dybbuk boxes aren't actually a real thing.[1] In fact, Kevin eventually came clean and admitted to making up the story. But it was too late, the wildfire had spread, and a vast majority of the paranormal field was eating it up. You can now find countless listings claiming to have "real dybbuk boxes" for sale, perpetuating the false narrative that these things are real. When, in fact, these are just boxes that sellers have made themselves to con you out of money. While a dybbuk is actually a spirit within Jewish folklore, the idea of a dybbuk box does not exist. I encourage you to research this topic and get your information from those who are actually in the Jewish community.

Now, on to the listings...

COMMUNICATES "DOWN BELOW"

$150 or best offer

Item is a red and black face statue that can be hung on the wall

Description: Only spirit I've come across who communicates with down below, yes you heard me correct. If you've ever wondered if your loved one made it above or below here is your chance. He is able to relay messages from down there. Do not be alarmed or offended to find out who has went to Hell. Just to be clear this is not a negative/demonic spirit just simply one who can go to that realm. His name is Frank and he has a very hoarse voice which makes him sound older but I'm unsure. Frank does not reveal his age. What I am able to tell is he was very heartbroken but puts up a tough front. Frank was not educated at all and made money the best he could to support the family. He would only get a few hours of sleep per night because of the work he did. His children and wife were always disrespecting him, it was never enough. He had a hard enough time trying to pay all the bills and then even worse being belittled. He began to drink very heavy. This then lead to his wife kicking him out of the home and still getting his money. Frank ended up in the streets which didn't seem bad at first. He would learn quickly the dangers of this sad but reality lifestyle.

HAUNTED CLOWN DOLL

Starting bid $300 or buy it now for $458

Item is a porcelain doll dressed as a jester

Description: This item is extremely haunted. Not for beginners. Please take this seriously. We keep it locked in the cubby at night and my son tied it up because it moves at night. We cannot always account for its whereabouts and my son finds it hard to accept that it does what it wants. It's been known to have stabbed the previous owner with a kitchen knife. He also kept it locked up. He gave it to us for our collection but we now have to let go of some of these items but we want to make sure they go somewhere where they can't harm someone. Please keep away from children and pets. We suggest you keep it in a locked case or cabinet after nightfall. Do NOT leave food with the doll. DO NOT ALLOW IT TO ACCESS OR BE IN KITCHEN. POSSESS AT YOUR OWN RISK. Item has been also known to cause possessions, poltergeist behavior and has been known to speak. Please keep away from children.

HAUNTED WITCH RING

Price of $250

Item is a 10 carat gold ring with garnet and pearls, size 6.5

Description: This ring was owned by a very powerful witch named Basheeba and tips the EMF meter off the scale. It's a very beautiful piece and can be worn with pride. Its prior owner was a loved local woman who practiced white magic. Basheeba was a local lady in her mid-seventies who was well-loved by all that came to know her. She practiced white magic, such as healing with herbs and positive spells to help the downtrodden, and in general, tried to show people that not all witches are bad. I knew her personally, and she taught me much about life.

She left me her estate when she passed, and it is full of wonderful things that magic still clings to. I've tried to find the right places for all her possessions, like her jewelry, as per her instructions. She wore many different rings of precious metals and stones of which I'm slowly finding new, worthy owners for.

Basheeba had only one person that I knew of who didn't like her, and that was a rival witch. The witch's name was Shirley, and she would call the city on Basheeba for anything and everything. The one thing that sticks out in time forever is "the war of the lawns," as the city called it. Any time Basheeba's lawn got out of hand due to not being maintained by mowing, Shirley would complain and try to get Basheeba fined by the city board for ordinance violations. Basheeba was not one to trot behind a lawn mower at 78 years old, and unless she found someone to mow it every week (like me,) Shirley was hot on the phone to the city complaining...

Finally, Basheeba grew so tired of this that she had all the grass removed and replaced the entire yard with wildflowers (or weeds) as they're commonly known. As it turned out, Shirley was deathly allergic to most of the new blossoms, but Basheeba's yard was now beautiful with 2-foot tall wildflowers everywhere, with absolutely no maintenance required. It made the front page of the newspaper in her city, and everyone laughed with a tongue in cheek at Basheeba's tormentor, who couldn't do a thing about her newfound predicament

Shirley sold her house and moved away the following spring. Both women are gone now, but Basheeba's wit and wisdom live on, along with her cleverly converted yard that has become a garden spot in her city. Her jewelry has absorbed her energy, and all that wear it claim to be able to feel the spirit of this wonderful witch, who helped all that came to her, and is sadly missed by all, including me. I wear two pendants of hers around my neck at all times and would never part with them. I can always feel their energy and Basheeba's presence nearby. I have many rings of solid 14kt gold, with beautiful gemstones set in them. They're all size 6 1/2, and all charged with a marvelous energy that heals, protects, and soothes the soul.

I hope this gives you somewhat of an idea of just how magnificent a human being Basheeba was.

DEMON ASCENSION RING

Starting bid of $88 or buy it now for $120

Item is an ornate silver ring with a sigil on it

Description: This stunning ring of DEMON ASCENSION will bring on the qualities and gifts of a DEMON. It will change, define, and categorize you higher in the ranks. You will ascend to the highest ranks if that is your wish and commitment. You will open up your life to a whole new world of possibilities and perspective. Any available rank will be yours as you rise up as an Earthbound Demon. This is a VERY POWERFUL EARTHBOUND DEMON SIGIL. Shortly after receiving the pendant, you will be told YOUR NEW NAME. This is when your BLESSINGS BEGIN... Full, complete instructions will be sent with the pendant. Ring is a men's size 12.

HAUNTED 1940S SWIVEL CHAIR

Price of $49

Item is an antique Domore chair

Description: I want this chair GONE, it is haunted by a spirit, even mentioned it to my friend Jimmy Church, Google him, he said welcome to my world. I bought this chair at a thrift store, and when I got it home we started noticing strange things, like a pewter platter we had on a shelf would just fall forward, and let me say it was leaning back, then our kids complained about random strange things, and everything started when the chair was brought home. It is not in our house anymore, and all the strange things stopped. Now you may say it is all talk, but to be honest I was laughing and saying no way, but my wife told me to take the chair out of the house, and all the strange things stopped. Now on to what the chair offers.

Overall the chair is in good vintage condition, all the wheels work, the seat covers appear to be synthetic, though they may not be, are pretty nice, the seat part does have a few cracks. This chair will or could use a restoration, the paint on it now is somewhat ugly and with a little work it could be a rather unique chair. BTW if you get the chair and have some strange things going on please don't return it. I am not joking when I said stuff was going on.

HAUNTED AVERY DOLL

Price of $36.29

Item is a blonde-haired porcelain doll wearing a green gingham dress.

Description: Avery died at the young age of 10 years old. She died from heart problems. She just couldn't fight anymore she was so tired of fighting. She told me she missed her whole family so much she wishes she would have kept fighting for them if not for myself she says. Avery loves to play with my other spirited children. One night after I first got her I could hear her banging on the walls and my husband wasn't home. And another night I could hear her walking around my house crying when I went to see who was crying I would see her laying on the floor and another night I could hear her walking up and down the basement stairs crying and again when I went to see what was wrong she was laying on the floor once again. She does keep asking me where she is and how she got there. She has just started talking to me without the spirit box. She told me she was sorry she was so shy and then she manifests in front of me. I asked her where she got this vessel, and she told me her mom brought it to the hospital one time when she went to visit. I am sorry I don't know a whole lot about her yet. But if any questions I will try to answer them the best I can.

HAUNTED ANTIQUE PHOTO

Price of $55

Item is an antique photo of a little girl

Description: Katelin (7) Haunted, very active, sweet, intelligent young lady, loves horses, wanted to be a famous cowgirl, loves children reading, being out in nature. Is a very driven little girl, who can do anything she puts her mind to. Her favorite offerings are cowgirl boots, a rope, and stuffed horses, she loves practicing her roping skills.

Was born to her single mother Phillis, who was a very strong but soft spoke women, her father left before she even had the chance to tell him she was pregnant, and she wasn't the type to chase a man. Her mother was a very hardworking waitress, she was often left home alone because her mother had to work a lot to support them, but their neighbors always kept an eye on her, and she was always out running around with the neighborhood children. One day while out running errands with her mother, she wasn't paying attention and got separated from her mom, a man had been watching her, and decided to grab her. She kicked and screamed and tried to get away. He was too strong, he threw her into the back of his car and took off. The police were alerted and were soon catching up to him, he ended up panicking and drove to a bridge where he threw her off, to get rid of her before the cops found him. He was soon caught but poor little Katelin did not survive the fall onto the rocks below.

Her vessel is this 4-inch sweet photo of her dressed up in her favorite cowgirl looking outfit. It was found among other photos in a vintage shop. Katelin's Activities: cold drafts, running, talking, apparitions, orbs, works well with trigger objects, dousing rods, pendulum, spirit apps, loves telling her story, enjoys spirit sessions.

ANTIQUE NEWS ARTICLE

While it may seem that the curiosity of haunted objects is a newer fad or interest for people, this is a topic that has been around for many, many years. Here is a news article I stumbled on that talks about an annoying spirit attached to a desk.

A HAUNTED DESK

Memphis Daily Appeal

March 11, 1883

The San Luis Obispo *Tribune* says that a very mysterious desk has for some time been an object of great solicitude in the office of the Pacific Coast railway. Several months ago Freight Agent Haskins observed a singular rapping and rattling noise in the desk at which he was writing, and endeavored to ascertain the cause. After a careful examination no cause could be found, and work was resumed. At very inopportune times this noise would be repeated, and a belief was aroused that spirits had taken possession of the desk and it was placed in another room. But even from there it continued its annoyance and it was sent down to the depot without any intimation of its tricks. But at the depot it continued its rappings, and the clerk to whom it was assigned chose boxes or tables or other desks to write upon rather than confess his fright at the haunted object which was his companion. Luckily a desk was wanted at the depot at Los Alamos. The clerk recommended that the one which had been assigned to him be sent, as he thought he could get along with it, and the officers of the company relieved him of the object of terror. The haunted desk was sent to Los Alamos, bearing a good character and a fresh coat of varnish. It was thought so great a removal would dislodge the troubled and troublesome spirit and give the clerks a rest. But now comes the complaint from Los Alamos of the mysterious noises from that same desk. What can be done with it? All are getting frightened. Cannot some medium investigate it and unravel the mystery, or send the desk on to Lompoc, where no spirits are allowed?

HOW TO CREATE A SPIRIT VESSEL (HAUNTED OBJECT)

An object is helpful with spirit work, as it can act as a physical anchor for a spirit, sort of like a midway point for the spirit to manifest in our physical realm, and gives us something tangible to focus on when connecting with the spirit. Technically anything can be used for a spirit vessel, such as a jar, a doll, jewelry, a crystal, a painting, etc. You might want to check with the spirit to see what kind of vessel they prefer. You can check with the spirit through divination or ask them to let you know in a meditation or dream.

I don't recommend anyone create a spirit vessel who doesn't have some sort of spiritual and magickal experience. It's important you are familiar with working with different energies and entities and are adept at banishing and protection work. Please respect spirits and don't go shoving spirits into objects for shits and giggles. Unless the spirit is okay with it, please don't make spirit vessels just to try to make a quick buck. This is a mutual agreement between you and the spirit. Make sure you are both aware of this commitment and the reasoning behind creating the vessel. Some believe the only exception to this is when it involves a malevolent spirit that might be causing you or someone else some serious harm. By binding the spirit to an object, theoretically it binds them from doing harm to anyone. By the malevolent spirit being in an object, you can then dispose of it properly or keep it locked away. I personally prefer a good old banishing ritual rather than forcing an entity into an object.

There are so many different types of spirit vessels and various bindings or ways to go about doing this. Ultimately it all depends on the type of spirit you're working with and what your ultimate goal is. For the sake of this book, and to keep it relatively user friendly regardless of your experience level, I'm including instructions on how to make a basic spirit vessel. Rather than binding the spirit to this item, essentially trapping it, the instructions here will help you create an anchor point for the spirit. This way, the spirit is able to come and go as they desire, but can use the object as a way to connect to the physical world. Think of it as a sort of safe space for the spirit when they're interacting with you or others.

Ideally you are doing this work with a spirit you're already familiar with. I absolutely do not recommend inviting any old random spirit into an object. You don't want to potentially open up your life to unsavory characters.

Once you have determined the object you're going to be working with, you want to physically and energetically clean it. Nobody wants to move into a dirty house, including spirits. Next, you can create a sacred circle if that is something you prefer to do. Place the object in front of you and set an offering nearby for the spirit. Hold your hands a few inches away from the object and say: I now consecrate this item as an anchor point and physical vessel for (say the spirit's name) to come and go as they please. Only (spirit's name) is permitted to inhabit this item; any other spirit or entity is blocked from entering this item. And so it is.

Keep your eyes closed and hands over the object, feeling and sensing the energy shift. You should be able to tell when the spirit has entered the vessel. Once it has, thank them, and the work is done.

Keep this object in a safe space and don't let others mess with it. This is essentially now a home or room for this particular spirit whenever they're visiting you, so treat it respectfully. Just like you would offer a living guest in your home food, water or conversation, do the same for the spirit. Remember, this particular working allows the spirit to come and go as they please. If you want them to actually hang around, you've got to pay attention to them.

You should now be able to interact with this item just as you would any other haunted item. Have fun, and be safe.

* * *

If you took pleasure in this book, please check out Cherise Williams' first book, *The Witch's Guide to Ghost Hunting*.

Please enjoy this excerpt:

HISTORY OF GHOST HUNTING AND THE ROLE OF THE WITCH

Tales of hauntings and spirits have been around for as long as there have been humans to encounter them. Ghosts are our connection to the other side. Communicating with them and learning exactly what they are could help us answer the greatest mystery of life: *what happens when we die?*

The popularity of ghost-hunting and paranormal reality television shows might make it seem as if ghost hunting is a newer activity. While the equipment and techniques we utilize on investigations today could be considered a little more modern, reaching out to the other side and searching for ghosts has been around for quite a long time.

A story that takes place in Athens, Greece, around AD 100 about a haunted home is considered by some to be an example of one of the first paranormal investigations, or ghost hunts. The residents of this home were supposedly so frightened by the paranormal activity that would occur there that they moved out. Athenodoros Cananites, a philosopher, rented the home with the hope of experiencing this activity for himself. He hoped to figure out a possible cause of this activity. While staying at the home, he saw the figure of an elderly man with a beard causing a ruckus with his clanking chains. Some even speculate that this is the origin of the classic depiction of ghosts with rattling chains. The story states that the ghostly figure directed Athenodoros to a spot on the floor. Athenodoros dug up the ground only to discover a body buried there. It's said that once the body was properly laid to rest, the haunting stopped. Based on this story, we can surmise that investigating the paranormal, at least on some level, has been around for almost two thousand years.

The ancient Greeks weren't the only ones to believe in ghosts and spirits. Literally every culture around the world and throughout history has mention of paranormal entities and stories of personal encounters to go along with them. It makes you think, if all of these different groups of people from all around the world all have stories and experiences relating to similar supernatural beings, there must be some truth to it.

In Europe, for a period of time, talking about the supernatural seemed to be fairly open and accepted. However, studies into the paranormal and acceptance of anything supernatural appear to wane during the rise of Christianity and the Church, especially around the 1500s. Almost anything that could fall into the paranormal category was seen as demonic, so most did not want to delve too deeply into the subject matter. When you add in all of the witch hunts and burnings, there weren't too many people willing to devote their studies or conversations to such a topic. Even though people weren't necessarily talking about these things out in the open, some were still studying and writing about them in private.

Around the early to mid-nineteenth century, people once again became more open about discussing and researching the paranormal. Big contributors to this openness were the Fox sisters and the rise of Spiritualism.

The Fox sisters, Kate and Maggie, lived with their parents in Hydesville, New York, in the mid-1800s. Supposedly living in a haunted home, Maggie and Kate decided to try to communicate with the ghost. They would ask a question, and in return there would be rappings on the walls in the form of an answer. For example, one knock for no, two for yes (a technique that modern ghost hunters still utilize today). The story of their haunted home and their ability to communicate with the ghost spread quickly. It wasn't long before the sisters were holding public séances, speaking with spirits. With the rise of their fame, more and more people began to announce their own mediumship abilities and hold séances themselves, most likely with the hope of money and fame coming their way.

While there were legitimate mediums, there were also many frauds. A lot of speculation was held around the Fox sisters in particular, with many people setting out to disprove their gifts. Unfortunately, the skeptics may have been correct, at least in regard to the Fox sisters. In 1888 Maggie Fox spoke with a reporter and explained how they had hoaxed the whole thing, and that they, in fact, were not communicating with spirits. A year later Maggie tried to recant her statement, but by then their reputation was ruined.

Even though the Fox sisters' reputation was tarnished, the belief in Spiritualism was still going strong and continues to this day. Spiritualism is a religious movement, with spirit communication being at the forefront.

With the rise of the Fox sisters, public séances, and Spiritualism, ghosts and the paranormal didn't seem quite as taboo as they once had. The topic continued to stay in the public, while more research and studies were conducted. More people began to seriously look into spirit communication and learning exactly what ghosts and hauntings are...or aren't. While there were lots of people who believed in Spiritualism, spirit communication, and mediums, there were a lot who didn't believe it either. Some made it their goal to document these occurrences, whether to prove or disprove what was happening. It could be said that this helped lay some of the groundwork for modern-day paranormal investigating, especially in regard to debunking activity and claims.

Some people think ghost hunting and the study of the paranormal is a bit woo woo and out there; however, ghost hunting has its roots in science. The story of philosopher Athenodoros is one example. The philosopher went to the haunted home with a plan of documenting the paranormal activity for knowledge and from a philosophical standpoint.

Another example of paranormal studies being rooted in science is the Society for Psychical Research (United Kingdom). The society was established in 1882 with the intention of approaching paranormal topics with a scientific and rational mind. In fact, author and researcher Catherine Crowe was a very large inspiration for the work of the SPR.

Catherine Crowe (Stevens) was born in Kent in 1790. She was a successful author and paranormal researcher. In 1848 her book *The Night-Side of Nature: or Ghosts and Ghost-Seers* was published. In this nonfiction book covering a wide array of paranormal experiences and theories, she mentions the now well-known paranormal terms *poltergeist* and *doppelgänger* and is credited as being the first person to bring these German terms to an English audience. She even theorized that poltergeists were likely caused by a human agent more often than a rowdy spirit, long before this was a widely accepted theory. Her book was so influential to the field that more than three decades after its release, the SPR would utilize many of her methods in their own research.[2]

Not only was she a successful author, but some call her the first ghost hunter and the Mother of the Paranormal. In her own investigations she utilized critical thinking and experimental tactics in order to study paranormal claims. She encouraged others not to dismiss the weird and unusual and instead to study it and look at it from an academic mind.

Some of the early members of the SPR were professionals in various scientific studies, such as professor of physics Balfour Stewart, chemist and physicist Sir William Crookes, renowned physicist Sir Oliver Lodge, and physiologist Charles Richet. The society has published countless research papers on various paranormal topics and continues to this day. Many were inspired by the work of the SPR, and other similar groups were formed to conduct research and investigate claims.

During more modern times with the rise of television and books being mass-produced, research into the paranormal became more mainstream. One investigator and researcher who really helped to change the face of modern ghost hunting was Hans Holzer. Hans Holzer was a parapsychologist and author who investigated countless claims of hauntings all around the world, writing well over a hundred books on the paranormal. His investigation style helped to inspire how a lot of ghost hunters conduct their investigations, even today. He was meticulous with his documentation of hauntings and enjoyed working with psychic mediums. He knew the importance of approaching hauntings and ghosts with both a scientific and psychic mindset.

THE ROLE OF THE WITCH

Witchcraft and ghosts have been associated with each other for about as long as either has existed. Perhaps it's because both witches and ghosts are considered things that dwell in the shadows, along with other creatures and beings. Or it could be it's due to the fact that for many years, the roles of communicating with the dead were primarily held by those considered to be witches. Communicating with spirits is something that many witches still practice today. With the connection of witchcraft and spirits (or ghosts), it makes sense that witchcraft and ghost hunting would correlate.

One of the most historically famous witches involved with spirit communication is the Witch of Endor. This story comes from the Old Testament, involving Saul, the first king of Israel. Even though witchcraft and necromancy (communing with spirits) was outlawed and punishable by death, some still practiced. Saul, worried about an impending battle with the Philistines, sought out the help of a sorceress who lived in Endor. After being reassured that she would not be punished for her work, the witch (who was unnamed) conjures the spirit of Saul's friend Samuel. Samuel then relays a message to Saul. The story of the Witch of Endor is not entirely unique. Witches throughout the ages have practiced necromancy, spirit conjuring, communication, and divination.

Most witches are at least somewhat familiar with the shadow realms, even if they don't actively reach out to spirits of the dead. To be a witch means to be in touch with the natural world, both seen and unseen. Witches have a certain understanding of energies, and they know how to connect to and work with those energies. Considering ghosts and other entities are a type of energy, it is only natural that witches would have an understanding of communicating with and sensing those entities. When reaching out to the other side and dealing with a haunting, who better to have along on a ghost hunt than a witch who has skills in spirit communication? A lot of witches are adept at sensing spirits and even relaying messages the entity might have. To me, that is a valuable trait to have in ghost hunting.

Not only are a lot of witches able to communicate with spirits, they're able to work with energy of all sorts. When investigating the paranormal, you are reaching out into the void. Nobody *really* knows what is on the other side. It's important to make sure that you are protected energetically when conducting investigations. Witches are able to sense and manipulate energy in many ways. For example, witches can cast spells for protection against negative entities, or a spell to help spirits communicate clearly through your ghost-hunting equipment. Witches are quite an asset when it comes to investigating the paranormal.

To continue reading *The Witch's Guide to Ghost Huntings*, please go to https://amzn.to/46Bj4uB.

Acknowledgments

THANK YOU

Thank you to my family for putting up with my crazy ideas and being so supportive of my writing. Thank you to everyone who took the time to share your personal stories and encounters with me; this book would quite literally not be the same without them. Thank you to everyone at Beyond the Fray Publishing for your patience and kindness. Thank you to Amy Parrish for helping me with some research. Thank you to Steve Overton of the Portland Puppet Museum. Thank you to all of the investigators and location owners whom I've had the pleasure to work with. And thank you, dear reader, for your time.

Notes

CHAPTER 2

1. https://www.atlasobscura.com/places/charles-dickens-door-and-haunted-mirror ; accessed November 30, 2022

CHAPTER 3

1. https://www.quesnelmuseum.ca/node/264; accessed March 23, 2023
2. https://sites.google.com/site/thingsmyanmar/myanmar-marionettes
3. https://www.burmalibrary.org/sites/burmalibrary.org/files/obl/docs21/Society%20and%20Culture/Patchareepan-Ravangban-2015-Nat_and_Nat_Kadaw_The_Existence_of_the_Local_Cult_in_Myanmar_Transition-en.pdf
4. https://www.burmalibrary.org/sites/burmalibrary.org/files/obl/docs21/Society%20and%20Culture/Patchareepan-Ravangban-2015-Nat_and_-Nat_Kadaw_The_Existence_of_the_Local_Cult_in_Myanmar_Transition-en.pdf
5. https://www.atlasobscura.com/places/charley-the-haunted-doll; accessed March 24, 2023

CHAPTER 5

1. https://www.stonehamstudios.com/haunted; accessed March 18, 2023

CHAPTER 12

1. https://www.jewitches.com/post/the-deal-with-the-dybbuk; accessed March 26, 2023
2. https://www.ameliacotter.com/2020/10/guest-post-first-ghost-hunter.html; accessed January 2022

About the Author

Cherise Williams is a paranormal investigator, researcher and tarot reader with over twenty years of experience. By pairing spirituality and witchcraft with a level-headed approach to the paranormal, Cherise has a unique perspective on the field. When she's not talking to spirits or pulling cards she enjoys being with her family, spending time in nature, and taking naps.

[f] facebook.com/CheriseWilliams.xo
[o] instagram.com/cherisewilliams.xo

Also by Cherise O. Williams

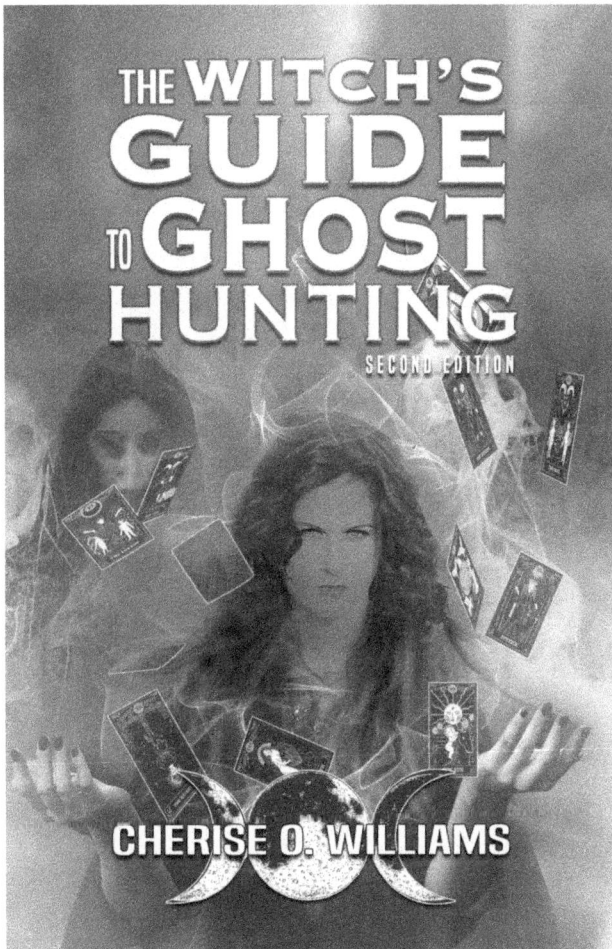

The Witch's Guide to Ghost Huntings

www.ingramcontent.com/pod-product-compliance
Lightning Source LLC
Chambersburg PA
CBHW032352280326
41935CB00008B/543